THE GREAT BRAIN
ROBBERY

£3 –

Gen

16/6.

"Lead us, Evolution, lead us
  Up the future's endless stair;
Chop us, change us, prod us, weed us,
  For stagnation is despair –
Gasping, guessing, yet progressing,
  Lead us nobody knows where.

To whatever variation
  Our posterity may turn –
Hairy, squashy or crustacean,
  Bulbous-eyed or square of stern –
Tusked or toothless, mild or ruthless –
  Towards that unknown goal we yearn.

Far too long have sages vainly
  Glossed great Nature's simple text;
He who runs may read it plainly:
  "Goodness = what comes next"!
By evolving, Life is solving
  All the questions we perplexed."

C. S. LEWIS, *"Poems"*,
Geoffrey Bles, 1964

THE GREAT BRAIN ROBBERY

by

DAVID C. C. WATSON

The use of Fashions in thought is to distract the attention of men from their real dangers....

so that nonsense in the intellect may reinforce corruption in the will.

C. S. Lewis (Screwtape)

ISBN 0 9514538 0 7

First published 1975

Reprinted 1976
Reprinted 1977
Reprinted 1982
Reprinted 1989

Typeset by University Printing Services
Printed in Great Britain
at the University Press, Cambridge

FOREWORD

V. Wright, M.D., F.R.C.P.,
ARC Professor of Rheumatology,
Co-Director Bioengineering Group
for the Study of Human Joints,
University of Leeds

The scientific community is in a ferment as regards evolution. The anniversary of Darwin's death saw a scathing denunciation of Darwinian evolution in The Times. The cartoon which accompanied this depicted the great man, clutching a copy of The Descent of Man, upturned on a banana skin surreptitiously placed beneath his feet by a monkey slinking away in the corner. The author's caustic comments were occasioned by the virtual absence of transitional forms in the fossil record, now freely acknowledged by palaeontologists. Despite the almost unbelievable richness of the fossil record, transitional forms have not been found. Great leaps are, therefore, postulated rather than the small graduations previously taught as established truth in our schools and universities – often accompanied by diagrams of geological columns showing these non-existent developments. This presentation of erroneous data, seen through prejudiced eyes, suggests that the forthright title of the present volume is well justified. As a scientist, it greatly concerns me that a fossil record which is now agreed to show large leaps should have been depicted as if it revealed small gradations. Yet it is a story that could be repeated ad nauseam in this field. When the village clock strikes 13 at noon, you distrust its previous pronouncements.

Many zoologists still cling to the evolutionary model, but they lag behind chemists and molecular biologists who are increasingly disillusioned by it. The analyses of astronomers such as Hoyle and Wickramasinghe, which show that the mathematical improbability of an evolutionary model taking place was so great as virtually to rule it out of court, are difficult to gainsay. They looked at the possible development of haemoglobin, the important constituent of red blood cells, and wrote, "The basic structures for the important biomolecules are mostly known, and calculations of their being formed through shufflings of the constituent atoms can be made. It turns out that a successful shuffling is a vastly more unlikely business than looking for the tiniest needle in the largest haystack". Commenting similarly on the development of enzymes, "The trouble is that there are about two thousand enzymes, and the chances of obtaining them all in a random trial is ... an outrageously small probability that could not be faced even if the whole universe consisted of an organic soup".

David Watson has rendered a considerable service by exposing the limitations of the evolutionary model and summarising the evidence for the creation model in 18 concise chapters. Anyone who has suffered in his professional career for his views, as David Watson has, deserves a hearing. That is even more so when the facts are on his side.

V. Wright,
October 1988.

DEDICATION

to Hannington Enoch
(d. April 1988)
Professor of Zoology in Madras University
and for many years
President,
Union of Evangelical Students
of India,
whose wisdom, friendship,
and Christian testimony
encouraged me to write this book

ACKNOWLEDGEMENTS

Dr. Morris and Prof. Whitcomb have kindly given me permission to quote extensively from their books. I believe that one day the whole Church will recognise the debt we owe them for their immense industry, zeal and wisdom in the cause of Christ.

I am also grateful to Professor James Barr of Oxford for recalling us to the straightforward traditional interpretation of Genesis (*Fundamentalism* ch 3, and *Escaping from Fundamentalism* ch 14). He clearly demonstrates the inconsistency of wresting Scripture to accommodate the 'assured results' of science.

CONTENTS

PART I

Chapters

PART II – REVIEWS

The Illustrated London News, 24th June 1922

THE EARLIEST MAN TRACKED BY A TOOTH: AN "ASTOUNDING DISCOVERY" OF HUMAN REMAINS IN PLIOCENE STRATA.

A PREHISTORIC COLUMBUS WHO REACHED AMERICA BY LAND?
AN ARTIST'S VISION OF HESPEROPITHECUS (THE APE-MAN OF THE WESTERN WORLD) AND CONTEMPORARY ANIMALS.

[Author's comment: Later the tooth was identified as belonging to an extinct pig.]

INTRODUCTION (1975)

"Crimes should be exposed not when they are being talked about but while they are being committed."

Alexander Solzhenitsyn

"This is a people robbed and spoiled." Isaiah

The Guinness Book of Records is a fascinating compilation. We are not surprised to find that the Train Robbery near Cheddington on 8 August 1963 was the Greatest ever. And the next page informs us of the Greatest Forgery: £150 million worth of £5 notes were printed by the German Government in 1940–41. The suggestion made in these pages is that another superlative should be added to the Record Book: the World's Greatest Delusion ("Brain Robbery") – EVOLUTION. For 100 years this Theory has darkened the intellect and dazzled the imagination of civilized man, but now at last the true light is dawning.

How is it that such a monstrous error could beguile so many millions of intelligent people for so many decades? The history of forging lends another illustration which may help us to understand. When in 1925 the notorious Alves Reis (later converted, and an outstanding Christian) counterfeited 500-escudo Portugese notes, he arranged that the printing should be done by Waterlows of London. His forgery went undetected for years because *the same plates were used to print the counterfeit notes as had been used to print genuine ones.* Similarly the Great Brain Robbery has gone undetected (except by very few) for years because the same word "evolution" is used to describe two absolutely distinct ideas – the one genuine, observable and true; the other spurious and false. Evolution F (for Fact) denotes "adaptation of a species within a species", which nobody would deny;

Evolution G (for Guesswork) denotes "The origination of species from earlier and totally different forms" (O.E.D.), which no one has ever observed. Because Evolution F has been proved, innocent students have assumed that Evolution G must be true.

The new Oxford Biology Readers (1973) furnish a good example of this confusion. In No. 55, "Evolution Studied by Observation and Experiment", Prof. E. B. Ford discusses the variation and adaptation of primroses, moths, butterflies and snails. This is Evolution *Fact*. On the other hand in No. 1, "Some General Biological Principles Illustrated by the Evolution of Man" by Sir Gavin de Beer, the same word is used to denote man's supposed origination from the lower primates. This is Evolution Guesswork. But because Prof. Ford's kind of evolution and Sir Gavin's have become inextricably confused in most people's minds, the counterfeit word has passed for genuine and civilization has fallen victim to the greatest Brain Robbery of all time.

No originality is claimed for these pages. Bigger and better books on the same subject have been written before. But since Evolution Guesswork continues to ravage our schools and wreck the faith of many, it is hoped that this small volume may cause Teachers, and trainers of Teachers, to think again.

PREFACE TO THE GREAT BRAIN ROBBERY
(1988 edition)

Predictably, this slim volume has had a mixed reception. No one was more surprised than I to find it named as one of the two "most important British books" on creation (Berry, GOD AND EVOLUTION, 1988). Some have objected to the title, on the grounds that it slanders evolutionists. But is this fair? Nobody blames Mr Mills for being the driver of the Great Robbery train: victims are not villains. Nor do we blame 18th century chemists for swallowing the phlogiston theory. We just think it was a pity they did not spot the error earlier.

I am encouraged to persist in my 'heresy' by the quotations in Appendix A, and by the following:

1) "I believe that one day the Darwinian myth will be ranked the greatest deceit in the history of science" — Soren Lovtrup, Professor of zoophysiology, University of Umea, Sweden, in DARWINISM: THE REFUTATION OF A MYTH (1987).

2) "Although Darwin's books are said to explain the origin of species, in fact they do no such thing" — Pearce Wright, Science Editor, 'The Times', reporting on the British Association for the Advancement of Science, Oxford, 30 August 1988.

3) "What is Darwin's theory of evolution but a far-fetched exercise in credulity that may well amuse posterity for generations to come?" — Malcolm Muggeridge, CONVERSION — A SPIRITUAL JOURNEY (1988).

Evidently a wind of change is stirring among the Olympians. Let it stir — "stormy wind, fulfilling His word"!

At the same time a number of Christian scientists are voicing their objections to creationism. In Part II I have tried to answer some of these. To me it seems that British evangelicals have been wandering in a wilderness for forty (literal!) years, cowed by the big names and big battalions of evolutionism. I invite them to think again: God is still on the side of the grasshoppers (Numbers 13.33).

David Watson
31 Harold Heading Close
CHATTERIS, Cambs. PE16 6TL

THE GREAT BRAIN
ROBBERY

PART I

"If there be a book in the whole Bible which purports to be a plain historical narrative of actual events, that book is the book of Genesis ... Why the first page of it is to be torn out, treated as a myth or an allegory, and in short explained away, — I am utterly at a loss to discover."

J. W. Burgon,
Fellow of Oriel College, Oxford, 1861

CHAPTER 1

PUZZLED PUPILS

"Mummy, if God did not mean what He said, why did He not say what He *did* mean?"

The little girl's question highlights a problem that has faced every teacher of Genesis over the past hundred years. From time to time theories "harmonizing" Science and Scripture have been put up by clever scholars and scientists, only to be shot down by equally clever scholars and scientists of the next generation – or even the next decade. Meanwhile the Christian public have been left to wander in the dark – vaguely hoping that, because some scientists are Christians, Science does not *really* contradict the Bible. By parity of reasoning one might conclude that, because many Hindus are scientists, Science does not really contradict Hinduism – although the Vedas teach that the moon is 50,000 leagues higher than the sun and shines with its own light, that the earth is flat and triangular, and that earthquakes are caused by elephants shaking themselves under it! No: the Christian conscience will not long rest satisfied with such questionable logic. That is why the wheel has now turned full circle, and an increasingly large number of people are beginning to wonder whether the "scientific" account of origins is the last word.

We live in an age of intense specialization. Knowledge has become so minutely subdivided that even at the Royal Society, so it is said, not more than 10% of the audience understand 50% of any lecture! 'Expertism' reigns, and a man's opinion on a subject is little valued unless he has graduated through the academic disciplines in that branch of learning. Now unfortunately the Bible – particularly Genesis – touches on a great number of sciences: anthropology, zoology, archaeology and philology to mention but a few. And who can claim to be an expert in more than one or two of these? Very few theologians have engaged in scientific research, and very few scientists have done more than dabble in Hebrew. Thus the interpretation of Genesis may be pronounced hopeless and abandoned at the start, because life is not long enough for anyone fully to grasp the intricacies of every Bible-related subject.

There is, however, another approach, indicated in Scripture itself. Almighty God wills that all men should be saved and come to the knowledge of the truth (I Tim. 2.4); He caused the Old Testament to be written for *our* learning and *our* admonition (Rom. 15.4; I Cor. 10.11); Christ said that till heaven and earth pass away, not one smallest part of any letter of any word of the Law (which includes Genesis) shall become obsolete. He also told some Hebrew scholars:

"Ye do err, not knowing the Scriptures, nor the power of God".

All this suggests that the key to Scripture (once translated) is a combination of *study* of related Bible passages, and *faith*. When these two are aligned, the lock opens. Conversely, when study and/or faith are lacking, God's secrets remain hidden, and the mind (however learned) gropes in darkness. The above-quoted verses also suggest that the God of the Bible would reveal the history of creation with such simplicity and clarity that the man-in-the-street of Tokyo, Timbuktu, or Tooting would not be deceived but would really understand whence he came and whither he goes.

The only God worthy of mankind's trust and adoration is the God who can accurately describe the world's past, as a basis for predicting the world's future. This is the very challenge which Jehovah makes to the gods of the heathen in Isaiah 41.22,23: "Declare ye the former things, what they be ... that we may know ye are gods"

(RV) The purpose of this book is to show that in Genesis we have an account of the creation of the world entirely satisfying, because it fits the facts of empirical science, and no other account can stand in competition with it. Perhaps, after all, God did say what He meant; perhaps He does mean exactly what He has said.

CHAPTER 2

FACING THE FACTS

"In fact the only natural exegesis is the literal one, in the sense that this is what the author meant ... he was deeply interested in chronology and calendar."

PROFESSOR JAMES BARR, *Fundamentalism* (1977)

Few books in the history of mankind can truly be called epoch-making: few books have radically changed the outlook and thinking of millions. In the past 500 years we might name Copernicus' "Revolutions of the Heavenly Spheres", Newton's "Principles", Karl Marx's "Rise of Capitalism" and Darwin's "Origin of Species" as among the most influential. It may well be that Morris & Whitcomb's "The Genesis Flood" (first published Feb. 1961) is worthy to be classed with such books.

The main drawback of "The Genesis Flood" is its length – though it had to be long and technical in order to convince the experts who might be expected to look for particular answers to the particular problems of their fields (such as geology and palaeontology). So it is the modest purpose of this writer to summarize the arguments by which Whitcomb and Morris have been led to the conviction that the first eleven chapters of the Bible are literally, historically, and scientifically true. Those who are not satisfied with the presentation given here are urged to buy "The Genesis Flood" and study it in detail.

Let us frankly admit that to an educated Christian the early chapters of Genesis present a harder intellectual problem than any other part of the Bible. Here he finds an account of the origin of the world totally different from what he has been taught at school and university, where the immense age of the earth and stars, and

Evolution, are assumed to be facts as undeniable as H_2O = water or twice two is four. If he consults the Encyclopaedia Britannica he will find these words:

"That the records of prehistoric ages in Genesis 1 – 11 are at complete variance with modern science and archaeological research, is unquestionable."

Secondly, Genesis 3.17-19 appears to teach that some drastic change came over the earth as a punishment for man's disobedience. Calvin comments: "The inclemency of the air, frost, thunders, unseasonable rains, drought, hail, and whatever is disorderly in the world, are the fruits of sin." But Science teaches that death, disease, famine and drought, thorns and thistles, and "Nature red in tooth and claw" have prevailed on this planet for scores of millions of years. The doctrine of the Curse has simply dropped out of the thinking of modern philosophers because no fossils have been discovered of straw-eating lions or vegetarian wolves! Once again there seems to be a head-on collision with the Bible.

Thirdly, Genesis 6-9 appears to teach that there was once a year-long Flood covering the whole globe; but in the Encyclopaedia Britannica we find this flatly denied:

"External evidence (i.e. Geology) recognizes no universal deluge ... Genesis preserves not literal history but popular traditions of the past ... many of the stories (other nations besides the Jews have Flood traditions) may arise from the inundations caused by the far-reaching tidal waves that accompany earthquakes .... Whenever flood-traditions appear to describe vast changes on the surface of the globe, these traditions are probably not the record of contemporary witnesses, but the speculation of much later thinkers". With this agrees the dictum of G. E. Wright in his "Biblical Archaeology" (1962): "The Flood is an exaggeration of a local inundation."

To sum up, in Genesis 1-11 we are faced with three

facts which the Bible appears very clearly to affirm, and which Science equally clearly denies:

1. The creation of the universe in six days of 24 hours.
2. The Curse on the earth.
3. The universal Flood.

It is now our purpose to show how Whitcomb and Morris have proved

a) that these doctrines are indeed taught in the Bible, and cannot be evaded;

b) that these doctrines are not contradicted by any *fact* of Science but only by the theories of scientists who base their whole philosophy on the false premise of Uniformitarianism.

Does the Bible teach a literal six day creation?

Obviously there is no point in defending a doctrine which God has not revealed, and many evangelical scholars would answer NO to the above question. Later, we shall examine some of their theories. But first let us look at the positive arguments for believing that the right answer is YES.

1. *The Demands of the Context.* The first reason for believing that the Bible teaches a literal six-day creation is this: the context demands it. The word for 'day' in Hebrew, as in many other languages, is used with a variety of meanings; but in nearly every case it is obvious from the context what is meant. In Genesis 1.5 the word is used to mean, first, day*light*, and secondly to include the hours of light *and* darkness. It seems very probable, therefore, that a 24-hour day is intended.

It has often been objected that, since the sun was not 'made' till the fourth day, the first three days at least cannot have been solar days. To this Calvin supplies the answer:

6

"It did not happen by accident that the light preceded the sun and the moon. To nothing are we more prone than to tie down the power of God to those instruments, the power of which He employs. The sun and moon supply us with light: and according to our notions we so include this power to give light *in them*, that if they were taken away from the world it would seem impossible for any light to remain. Therefore the Lord, by the very order of the creation, bears witness that He holds in His hand the light, which He is able to impart to us without the sun and moon".

2. *The use of the word 'day'*. Secondly, in nearly every other Old Testament passage where 'days' is used with a numeral, it means literal days of 24 hours. The only possible exceptions are Daniel 8.14 and 12.11,12; but these chapters are visions, a type of literature entirely different from Genesis One, which bears all the marks of being "sober history" (E. J. Young). (Professor Young was recognised as one of the world's most eminent Hebrew scholars of the '50s and '60s).

There is an interesting parallel to Genesis 1.1–2.4 in Numbers 7, where we read that "the princes offered for the dedication of the altar *in the day* that it was anointed". We might have thought that all offered on the same day, had not the narrative gone on to inform us that they offered on twelve separate days. We have "the first day .... second day .... etc." exactly as in Genesis One; and common sense tells us that the word 'day' is used in Numbers 7.10 with a comprehensive meaning, while in the rest of the chapter it is used literally to denote a period of 24 hours. Similarly common sense tells us that in Genesis 2.4 'day' is used with a comprehensive meaning, summing up the six individual and literal days of the previous chapter.

3. *The Fourth Commandment*. Thirdly, God's com-

mentary in Exodus 20 states that God's working week and man's working week are exactly parallel:

"Six days shalt thou labour .... for in six days the LORD made heaven and earth, the sea, and all that in them is ...."

E. J. Young comments: "The fourth commandment actually refutes the non-chronological interpretation of Genesis One". Let us remember, too, that there is no possiblity of the Ten Commandments being man's interpretation of God's word. If any part of the Bible is verbally inspired, this must be, since we are told it was the writing of God written with the finger of God on tablets which were the work of God (Exodus 31.18;32.16). Dr Marcus Dods (1900) wrote: "If the word 'day' in this chapter (Genesis One) does not mean a period of 24 hours, the interpretation of Scripture is hopeless."

For at least two generations this commandment has caused acute embarrassment to the friends of Christianity, and glee to her foes. The situation may not inaptly be compared to a hypothetical scene at Greyfriars School where a Prefect is showing a new boy round. Coming to the Headmaster's study door they find engraved upon it in letters of gold the Ten School Rules:

1. Mr Topman is the only authorised Headmaster.

2. No boy shall draw any picture of the Headmaster.

3. No boy shall call the Headmaster by any nickname.

4. No boy shall read by moonlight, because the Man in the Moon might be offended.

5. Every boy shall write to his parents once a week.

etc.

New Boy: They all seem reasonable enough, except for Number Four. What on earth does he mean by that? You don't mean to say the Headmaster really believes in the Man in the Moon? That's just a fairy tale!

8

Prefect: Well – er – um – yes, perhaps. But some boys think there must be some deep hidden meaning to the Rule ... anyway, there is a long-standing tradition at Greyfriars that we don't read by moonlight.

New Boy: Well, I think it's ridiculous! A Head who puts a statement like *that* in the middle of his rules doesn't deserve to have *any* of them obeyed!

Similarly, thousands of Bible-readers have dismissed all Ten Commandments as an antiquated tribal code unfit for 20th century man, because of this 'totally unscientific concept' annexed to the Fourth. (Alan Dale's "Winding Quest", 1974, omits verse 11 altogether in his paraphrase of the Mosaic Covenant). How very *unwise* of God to set all morality at risk by thrusting such a bald, bold, ridiculous statement in the middle of His otherwise reasonable laws – ridiculous, that is, *unless after all it is true!*

4. *The Interpretation of Older Commentators.* The fourth reason for believing that the days of Genesis One are literal 24 hour days is this: the vast majority of Jewish and Christian scholars down the ages have believed them to be so. Origen, it is true, thought they might represent ages; but since there is nothing whatever in the text of Scripture to support this idea, it died a natural death. We have already quoted Calvin. The Shorter Catechism (1647) reads:

Q. What is the work of creation?

A. The work of creation is, God's making all things of nothing, by the word of His power, in the space of six days, and all very good.

Thomas Scott's Commentary (1780) usually mentions varying interpretations where they exist, but he says nothing about any possibility of the 'days' being other than 24-hour days. Only since the middle of the 19th century, when geologists began dogmatically to assert the immense antiquity of the earth, have Christians begun to doubt. Thus Keil & Deilitzsh (1875) know of other views, but emphatically reject them: "If the days of creation are regulated by the interchange of light and darkness, they must be regarded not as periods of time of incalculable duration, or of thousands of years, but as simple earthly days." Professor S. R. Driver examines and refutes all the attempts to reconcile Genesis One with the dogmas of Science, and concludes: "Verses 14–18 cannot be legitimately interpreted except as implying that, in the conception of the writer luminaries had not previously existed; and that they were 'made' and 'set' in their places in the heavens *after* the separation of sea and land ....." Finally, the German scholar Gerhard von Rad in his monumental Commentary on Genesis (1960) writes as follows: "Unquestionably the days are to be regarded as literal days of 24 hours." (Both Driver and von Rad would explain the Six Day Creation as a mistaken and primitive idea: we call on them only as acknowledged linguistic experts to tell us what the original writer *meant*. Whether or not the original writer's idea was *true* is another question, which will be discussed later).

5. *The Failure of Modern Commentators.* The fifth reason for believing that the days of Genesis One are literal days is this: all attempts to explain the early chapters of Genesis as anything other than "sober history" have, sooner or later, been proved inconsistent, incoherent, or erroneous. The "explanation" often poses more problems than it solves, as the following examples will show:

Is it symmetrical?

(a) Many writers have tried to discover a 'symmetry' in Genesis One which would enable them to call it poetry and to interpret it non-literally and non-chronologically. E. J. Young (p. 55 ff.) has shown this view to be untenable; but the 'New Bible Dictionary' actually printed a diagram demonstrating that fishes were made on the *sixth* day (the Bible says the fifth) in order to prove a correspondence with the creation of the sea on the third day! The comment here of Keil and Delitzsch is still very much to the point:

"The creation of fish and fowl on the same day is an evident proof that a parallelism between the first three days of creation and the last three is not intended and does not exist ... the account before us is obviously a historical narrative."

Is it poetry?

(b) Others have called Genesis One a 'Hymn of Creation', in which we may expect to find poetical metaphors and spiritual ideas clothed in figurative language. But Hebrew poetry has a character as definite as Homeric hexameters or Shakesperian sonnets: its main features are parallelism and repetition, which we find even in the first 'poem' of the Bible (Gen. 4.23,24). And parallelism and repetition are conspicuously absent from Genesis One, so we cannot call it poetry. Compare, for example, Psalm 33:

"By the word of the Lord were the heavens made,
And all the host of them by the breath of His mouth.
He gathereth together the waters of the sea as an heap:
He layeth up the deeps in storehouses."

Here each idea is repeated in different words: this is poetry. Now Genesis One:

11

"And God said, Let there be light, and there was light
...

And God said, Let the waters under the heaven be gathered together into one place, and let the dry land appear: and it was so".

No parallelism, no repetition: this is history. (Admittedly v.27 is repetitious, but notice that the *same* verb is used three times. This kind of repetition is hardly ever found in Hebrew poetry.)

Is a harmony possible between Genesis and Science?

(c) Many have tried to prove that the geological time scale agrees with the order of creation in Genesis One, and for years this was confidently asserted by Christian apologists. However, this line of defence too has had to be abandoned (see ch. 3). A recent booklet (published by Crusade magazine, May 1967) which attempts to propagate this mistaken idea is 'The Origin of Man' by Victor Pearce. He suggests that we have evidence of Man's Age of Innocence in the "First Danubians" of prehistoric Central Europe, because they had no weapons or fortifications. Canon Pearce seems to overlook the fact that Adam and Eve were *fallen* creatures when they were cast out of Eden, and before they had any children. They could scarcely have begotten a tribe of "innocent" nomads. In the very next chapter of Genesis we meet murder and the words 'slay', 'smite', 'wound' and 'bruise'. There was violence enough in the world, it suggests, long before any migrations to Europe; and the Bible clearly teaches that *only* Adam and Eve were ever innocent, and *only* in Eden. All the artefacts of 'early man' must have belonged to Eve's posterity, who were fallen, sinful creatures, condemned (as we are) to toil for a living, and inclined (as we are) to fight one another. But

12

probably then, as now, some tribes were less bellicose than others.

Is the seventh day still incomplete?

(d) Another theory is that, because no evening or morning are mentioned in connection with the seventh day, therefore God's 'sabbath' is still continuing after many thousands of years; hence each of the six days may represent an equally long and indefinite period. But this theory does not fit the words of Scripture, which are: "He rest*ed* on the seventh day ... and God blessed the seventh day because in it He rest*ed*." The basis of all theology is Grammar, and Grammar distinctly tells us here that God's resting was in the Past Definite tense, not in the Present Continuous. Exodus 31.17 says the same: "He rested and *was* refreshed": so does Hebrews 4.10: "... himself also rested from his works as God *did* (rest) from His." We conclude, then, that God's rest was for 24 hours, exactly as man's should be. We must correct our ideas of God from Scripture, not correct Scripture in order to make it suit our ideas of God.

Is there a gap between Genesis 1.1 and 1.2?

(e) This "Gap Theory" was popularized by the Scofield Bible and is still believed by not a few. Verse two is translated, "and the earth *became* waste and void...", and this is supposed to refer to some judgement of God on the 'pre-Adamite' earth. Because in Exodus 20.11 the word is "made", not "created", Genesis One is interpreted as a restoration of the earth, not the original creation.

On linguistic grounds the theory has been refuted both by E. J. Young and F. F. Bruce ('Transactions of the Victoria Institute' 1946, p. 21), but its error will be apparent even to those who have only the AV. Can we distinguish between 'created' and 'made' in Genesis One? The answer seems to be No, except in v.1 where 'created' must mean 'created out of no pre-existent materials'. Let us examine the other verses where one or other of the words is used:

vv.6,7: "Let there be a firmament ... and God *made* the firmament."

vv.14–16: "Let there be lights ... and God *made* the two great lights."

vv.20–21: "Let the waters bring forth ... and God *created* the great sea-monsters."

vv.24/25: "Let the earth bring forth ... and God *made* the beast of the earth."

vv.26/27: "God said, Let us *make* man ... and God *created* man, in the image of God *created* He him; male and female *created* He them."

v.31: "God saw everything that He had *made*."

Here we may note (1) It is rather hard to maintain that the process of "creating" sea-monsters was different from that of "making" the beasts: in both cases there was pre-existent material. (2) The verses about Man show that the two words must be considered synonymous in the context. (3) If "made" in Genesis 1.31 can include three acts of creation (vv. 1, 21, 27) – as it obviously does – there seems little reason to doubt that in Exodus 20.11 it can do the same.

Genesis 2.7 uses yet a third word – "formed" – to describe the creation of Man; but a comparison with Isaiah 45.7 shows that all three words are sometimes synonymous. In Genesis One and Two they denote not three different processes but the *same* process viewed from three different angles, for variety and emphasis.

(f) A most ingenious attempt to escape from the literal interpretation of Genesis One is found in Derek Kidner's

Commentary (June 1967). Mr. Kidner suggests that the "latent truth" of the chapter (six days = 15 billion years) was hidden from Moses, just as Daniel did not know the full import of the words spoken to him – "I heard, but I understood not" (Daniel 12:9) – and Peter says that the prophets did not know the time when Christ would suffer (I Peter 1:10). Will this analogy hold water?

First let us notice that, though Daniel and Isaiah may not have entirely understood what they were commanded to write, they certainly knew they were writing prophecy (Peter says it was *revealed* to them). But in Genesis One there is nothing to suggest that we are reading a prophecy. There is nothing to suggest that Moses did not perfectly understand what he was writing about Creation, just as he perfectly understood what he wrote about Joseph. The author evidently regarded the 'origin' of the heaven and earth in exactly the same way as he regarded the 'origin' of Abraham, Noah and the rest – as literal history of the past.

Secondly, one important purpose of Biblical prophecy seems to be that after the event God's people may be able to show others how He has manifestly fulfilled His own words. This was certainly achieved in the case of Daniel's prophecies – so marvellously that sceptics and Higher Critics still maintain they were written *after* the event! Isaiah 53, too, was exactly fulfilled in the life, death and burial of Christ. The Apostles could point with utmost confidence to that chapter as proving the extraordinary fact that the Messiah *must* suffer; and Apollos "powerfully confuted the Jews, and that publicly, showing *by the Scriptures* that Jesus was the Christ" (Acts 26.23; 18.28).

Now in the case of Genesis One, could a modern Christian "powerfully confute" unbelievers by proving from the Scriptures that the scientific understanding or Evolution was stated therein thousands of years before

Darwin? We might imagine the posters for a public lecture:

THE BIBLE IS TRUE

SIX DAYS = 15 BILLION YEARS!

GEOLOGY CONFIRMS GENESIS,

THOUGH TOTALLY DIFFERENT!

This is indeed 'reductio ad absurdum'. As everyone knows, Genesis has been the laughing-stock of unbelievers for a hundred years. So far from any 'prophecy' in it being fulfilled, almost every word of the chapter has been held up to ridicule as contradicted by the "assured results of geology". So far from anyone coming to believe Genesis through seeing its 'fulfilment', millions of high-school and university students have been turned aside from reading the Bible because they found in Genesis One an impassable *stumbling-block* to faith. How then can this chapter be regarded as prophecy, the purpose of which is to *strengthen* faith by an exact correspondence between the prediction and the event?

Conclusion

No: if we are to justify the inclusion of Genesis One in the Bible, it cannot be as prophecy any more than as poetry, parable, or picture. When God has told us that He made the universe in six days, and in a certain definite order, adding a precise chronology, it seems rather presumptuous to state that 'the Bible only answers the question By whom? and not the questions *How* or *When* was the world made?' We must unflinchingly face the fact (in the words already quoted) "that the records of

16

prehistoric ages in Genesis 1–11 are at complete variance with modern science and archaeological research". If Science is right, then the Bible is wrong: if the Bible is right then Science is wrong.

CHAPTER 3

THE ORIGIN OF THE UNIVERSE

"Where were you when I laid the foundations of the earth?"   Job 38.4

A question that some may be asking is this: on a scientific matter, of what value is the opinion of anyone who is not a scientist? Should we not leave all such investigations to the experts, and meekly accept their conclusions?

To answer this we must ask another question: What is Science? By definition it means *knowledge*, which can refer only to facts discovered by observation, experiment, or trustworthy testimony. So long as a scientist tells us what he or others have observed with their own eyes, or what he or others can reproduce by experiment, we shall be satisfied that he is telling us *facts*. We accept that water is H_2O because we are assured that experiments have proved it to be so. But when a man believes something not on the basis of observation or experiment or trustworthy testimony, he ceases to act as a scientist and begins to theorize as a philosopher. For instance most scientists believe in Evolution, in spite of the enormous gaps in the fossil record. They have not observed Evolution, neither can they reproduce it by experiments; they believe it has taken place because it *seems* to them more probable than Special Creation. But this is not true science: it is faith in the unseen.

One of the chief reasons for assigning to the universe an age of about 15,000 million years is the time required for light to travel from the more distant stars. The argument runs:

1. Distance from the earth to star A = 1000 million light years.

2. We can see this star's light.

3. Therefore the light from star A must have begun travelling toward us at least 1000 million years ago.

4. Therefore star A must have appeared in the sky at least 1000 million years ago.

But the whole argument breaks down if at step (3) we introduce the God of the Bible. "Why could not God in the twinkling of an eye have formed the stars so that their light could be seen from the earth?" (E. J. Young). God is not subject to the laws He has made for the normal running of the universe.

Suppose some chemists were to fly back in a Time Machine to Cana in Galilee in A.D. 26, to a house where a wedding is in progress. Analysing the wine being drunk at the end of the feast they would report: "This wine appears to be thirty years old, judging by the speed of fermentation which we observe today in ordinary grape-juice." Their observation would be perfectly correct. But suppose they go on to say, "This wine *must* be thirty years old because the speed of fermentation can never be changed", they would be wrong. Now they speak no longer as scientists but as philosophers, denying that God could or would ever break His own speed limit. (See John's Gospel, ch. 2.)

The point will bear repetition. We shall now send our Time Machine chemist to a hill by the Lake of Tiberias in A.D. 27. Here he is asked to analyse some barley bread. The report might be: "This bread appears to have been made from barley flour mixed with water and yeast; the flour was produced by grinding barley corn which had grown for six months and had then been cut, threshed and stored." But if he further asserts that the bread could not have been produced in any other way, the crowd of five thousand men would retort: "We saw Jesus of Nazareth make the bread with His own hands in (practically) no time. Almighty God is not dependent on the methods which He usually employs. Keep your chemistry for the ordinary processes of life, but don't attempt to analyse miracles!" (See John 6.)

Similarly, so long as the astronomer is content to record present processes, distances and movements, we may respect and admire his marvellous instruments and complex calculations. But if he proceeds to tell us that God never could or would have acted otherwise than in accordance with processes and speeds *now* observed, we may justly point out that this is not an objective statement of fact but a mere opinion, no less fallible than any other human opinion.

In Hebrews 11 we read: "Through faith we understand that the worlds were framed by the word of God, so that things which are seen were not made out of things which do appear." The miracle spoken of here was even greater than either of the two mentioned above. Christ incarnate, the Redeemer, used water to make wine and bread to make more bread; but Christ transcendent, the Creator, used *no* pre-existent material to form the universe as we now see it. Genesis One shows us a fully running world, with an apparent age, created in six days. Just as Christ at Cana compressed into one second the process of thirty years, so in one day He flung the stars billions of light-years into space, at the same time causing their light to fall upon the earth. How do we know? Because He says so!

Still pursuing this question of "apparent age", let us send our Time Machine man (a physiologist this time) to the Garden of Eden on the sixth day of creation. Applying his height and weight charts to Adam and Eve he might deduce that they appear to be fully developed adults about, say, 25 years old. If he goes on to say that they *must* have been alive for 25 years, that they must have been born as he was born, we have a right once more to reply: "Now you speak not as a scientist but as an unbeliever. God says He made Adam and Eve as full-grown adults; and God can do *anything*." So it is in regard to the stars: they all have an "apparent age" which the scientist can measure. But to assert that this is their *actual* age – that they must have been "born" in this way or that way millions of years ago – is to dogmatize quite outside the realm of Science.

What is Faith?

When Noah was told that a Flood was coming he did not start measuring the quantity of water in the atmosphere, or the rainfall of Mesopotamia. He did not work out scientifically how such a thing could happen: he simply believed the word of God. When Joshua was told that the walls of Jericho would fall down he did not consult a seismograph or study the statics and dynamics of Canaanite engineering: he simply believed the word of God. So, surely, according to our text (Heb. 11.3) faith in creation means a simple acceptance of the statement: "God made two great lights ... He made the stars also ... and the evening and the morning were the fourth day."

Looking more closely at 'faith' in Hebrews 11 we shall find that in every case it was exercised in regard to matters of which the believer had no previous experience. Enoch had never seen anyone "disappear" to be with God; Noah had probably never seen rain (Gen. 2.5); Moses had never seen the Red Sea divide. They believed in the "impossible", because God said it would happen. Similarly creation-out-of-nothing has always seemed impossible to unregenerate man, from the most primitive to the most highly civilized. The Thlinkit Indians of North America believed that a creator-hero stole the sun, moon and stars out of a box, and hung them up to illuminate the earth. Plato taught that matter is eternal, and that all

21

visible things came out of other visible things. This shows the vital importance of Hebrews 11.3: only by personal faith in a personal Creator will anyone ever believe what the world has always deemed impossible – that "it pleased God to create, or make out of nothing, the world and all things therein, whether visible or invisible, in the space of six days" (Shorter Catechism).

CHAPTER 4

"A THOUSAND YEARS AS ONE DAY"

"We need to remember that limitless time is a poor substitute for that Omnipotence which can dispense with time. The reason the account of creation given here is so simple and so impressive is that it speaks in terms of the creative acts of an omnipotent God, and not in terms of limitless *space and* infinite *time and* endless *process."*

Professor O. T. Allis ('God Spake by Moses')

In the early days of the Bible-Science controversy, Christian apologists often had recourse to II Peter 3.8 as an explanation of the Six Days of creation. They maintained that the 'Record of the Rocks' tends to confirm the biblical order. Genesis One, they thought, could still be interpreted as a chronological *sequence* even though each 'day' must represent many million years. There still remained the perplexing problem of the heavenly bodies, which are said to have been "made" on the fourth day; but this was solved by interpreting "made" as "made to appear", notwithstanding the very slender linguistic evidence upon which this translation is based ("that the heavenly bodies were made on the fourth day, and that the earth had received light from a source other than the sun, is not a naive conception but a plain and sober statement of the truth", E. J. Young p. 95).

However, a glance at the Geological Time Scale as given in the Encyclopaedia Britannica 1971 (article 'Geology'), alongside the Genesis sequence, reveals the impossibility of thus reconciling Science with Scripture:

System & Period	Distinctive Records of Life	Began	Genesis
	I. CENOZOIC ERA	(Milions of Years Ago)	
	(total 70m. years)		
Quaternary	Early Man	2+	Day 6
Tertiary	Large carnivores	10	Day 6
	Whales, apes	27	Day 5, 6
	Large browsing animals	38	Day 6
	Flowering plants	55	Day 3
	First placental mammals	65–70	Day 6
	II. MESOZOIC ERA		
	(total 155m. years)		
Cretaceous	Extinction of dinosaurs	130	
Jurassic	Dinosaurs' zenith		
	primitive birds		Day 5
	first small mammals	180	Day 6
Triassic	Appearance of dinosaurs	225	Day 6
	III. PALAEOZOIC ERA		
	(total 345m. years)		
Permian	Conifers abundant		Day 3
	Reptiles developed	260	Day 6
Carboniferous			
upper	First reptiles		Day 6
	Great coal forests	300	Day 3
lower	Sharks abundant	340	Day 5
Devonian	Amphibians appeared		
	fishes abundant	405	Day 5
Silurian	Earliest land plants		
	and animals	435	Day 3, 6
Ordovician	First primitive fishes	480	Day 5
Cambrian	Marine invertebrates		
	(shellfish etc.)	550–570	Day 5
	IV. PRE-CAMBRIAN ERA		
	(total 2920m. years)		
No known basis for systematic division	Plants and animals with soft tissues	3490	Day 5

****

	Began	Genesis
Origin of the Earth	4500(?)	Day 1
Origin of Solar System	?	Day 4

In the above table note that (a) the grand divisions are *not six but four*. Even if we include the era before the Earth was "born", that still makes only five divisions; (b) *no two divisions are the same length*, and the first (pre-Cambrian) is forty times as long as the last (Cenozoic). It is hard to see how these four or five periods vastly differing in length could be adequately represented by six equal "days"; (c) the order of events coincides at one or two points, but in general is *very different* in the two columns.

Thus it seems that Kidner's optimism – "a remarkable degree of correspondence can be found between this sequence and the one implied by modern science" ('Genesis', p. 55) – is scarcely justified by the facts. The true solution may lie in another direction: "this uniformitarian, evolutionary scheme of historical geology is basically fallacious" ('The Genesis Flood' – hereafter referred to as TGF – p. 136); and "the geological column is an artificial composite affair, with the strata arbitrarily arranged according to the nature of their fossil content to tell the story of evolution ... there is no spot on earth to which one can go and see more than a few thousand feet of stratified rocks. And in not one of these places can the evolutionary story of any animal or plant be seen" (Professor H. Enoch, 'Evolution or Creation?' p. 27).

What, then, does the Apostle mean by "one day is with the Lord as a thousand years, and a thousand years as one day"? He is preparing the Christian Church for a long delay before the Saviour returns, and with prophetic insight he suggests that it may extend even to (a few) thousands of years. He refers to the *literal* millennia of *human* history, not to the fabulous aeons of pre-history. Bible words do not, like mathematical symbols, possess a fixed value, so that one phrase can be picked up from any passage and dropped into any other, while still retaining its identical meaning. To toss II Peter 3.8 into the middle of Genesis One is about as sensible as to affirm that Matthew 27.63 means, "After three thousand years I shall rise again".

In passing we may note that the error of scientists in regard to the *past* age of the universe leads them into an equally serious delusion concerning the *future*. Fred Hoyle, ex-Professor of Astronomy at Cambridge, states: "As the sun steadily grills the earth it will swell ... until it swallows the inner planets one by one: first Mercury, then Venus, then possibly the earth. This particular idea of the New Cosmology seems to fit in well with mediae-val ideas of Hell ... after 5000 million years our galaxy will stop growing. Then what? I should very much like to know." He concludes: "The cosmology of the Hebrews is only the merest daub compared with the sweeping gran-deur of the picture revealed by modern Science. This leads me to ask the question: Is it reasonable to suppose that it was given to the Hebrews to understand mysteries far deeper than anything we can comprehend, when it is quite clear that they were ignorant of many matters that seem commonplace to us? No, it seems to me that religion is but a desperate attempt to find an escape from the dreadful situation in which we find ourselves ... we still have not the smallest clue to our own fate" ('The Nature of the Universe', pp. 35, 95, 100, 103).

Professor Hoyle can afford to be dogmatic in his "scientific" predictions of the future because he knows that the whole civilized world has accepted the "scien-tific" explanation of the past. But it may be hoped that Christians who read his words will realize that, once we abandon the literal interpretation of Bible history, *there is no limit to unbelief.* If 'day' does not mean day in Genesis One, there is no reason why 'hell' should mean hell or 'heaven' mean heaven in Revelation 21. The children of this world are wiser in their generation than the children of light: they clearly perceive that if Genesis be not a true account of the beginning of the world, there is no reason why Revelation should be considered a true account of the end of the world. The whole Bible stands or falls together, and in the eyes of the world it has fallen – the basis smashed to smithereens. But how firm a foundation has been laid, by the New Cosmology, for the New Theology and New Morality!

CHAPTER 5

SCIENTIFIC PREJUDICE

"If you have hitherto disbelieved in miracles, it is worth pausing a moment to consider whether this is not chiefly because you thought you had discovered what the story is really about? – that atoms and time and space ... were the main plot? And is it certain you were right?"

C. S. LEWIS, '*Miracles*'

It is now time to turn our attention to the men who have produced theories of the Origin of the Universe, and enquire what leads them to deny the validity of the Genesis record. Such scientists are known as 'cosmogonists'. At this point an illustration may help. Suppose an ardently patriotic and anti-American Frenchman were to write a History of Aviation. Having traced the story back to Bleriot's cross-Channel flight in 1909, he wishes to maintain that the French were the first to invent a flying-machine. Therefore he sits down at his drawing-board and sketches a number of imaginary planes which *might* have preceded Bleriot's. Being an expert mathematician and engineer he can argue in a very plausible way that each of these hypothetical machines is an advance on the previous one; that each of them obeys the laws of aeronautics; and that therefore the evolution and invention of the first flying-machine by the French is certainly possible. If it is possible, then it is probable. If probable, then practically certain. By repeating his claims over and over again, with an impressive display of mathematical detail, our Frenchman might succeed in convincing his fellow-countrymen (many of whom might share his anti-American prejudice) that the honour and glory of inventing the first aeroplane are due to the French! In fact, of course, the first flight was made by the American Wright brothers at Kitty Hawk, North Carolina, on December 17, 1903. The historical record is unimpeachable, and no amount of theorizing, speculation, or drawing-board pictures, can ever disprove it.

Now I believe that the modern cosmogonist is not unlike that Frenchman. Thoroughly indoctrinated with the Theory of Evolution, he rules out all possibility of Genesis One being literally true.

He settles down at his astronomical 'drawing board' and produces, with impressive mathematical detail, a series of hypothetical explosions and contractions, gyrations and convolutions, which *might* have led up to the formation of the heavenly bodies as we now observe them. He writes a book on the subject, which is soon followed by another, then another, as he increasingly persuades himself and others that his drawing-board 'creations' *actually happened!* After ten or twenty years his world fellow-citizens (many of whom are equally unwilling to accept God's revelation) forget all about the historical record in Genesis. They come to see the drawing-board theories first as possible, then probable, then as practically certain. If other equally learned astronomers produce other and totally different designs, that matters little. Somehow or other, Science has "disproved" the Bible!

Here we may note a strange anomaly. Science itself – and not least astronomy – depends on historical records. Edmund Halley, who assisted Isaac Newton, discovered the comet subsequently called "Halley's Comet" by comparing the written records of 24 comets observed from 1337 to his own day (1704). He found that four comets had moved in practically identical paths (1456, 1531, 1607, and 1682, i.e. at intervals of about $75\frac{1}{2}$ years). He therefore correctly assumed that the four appearances belonged to one body, whose return might be expected about 1758. This prediction was justified by the event: the comet returned in 1759 and again in 1835 and 1910. The important thing to notice is that every one of these appearances apart from the last (which was photographed) is known to us now only *by the written testimony of reliable witnesses*. This is real Science: knowledge based upon observation and the observer's testimony.

CHAPTER 6

WHITCOMB'S 'ORIGIN OF THE SOLAR SYSTEM'

"... there is no theory of stellar evolution that will make Sirius change from red to blue-white in 2000 years. I would much prefer to learn stellar evolution from the ancient myths of man than from the modern myths of the computer."

KENNETH BRECHER, *Astronomy of the Ancients*,
(Mass. Inst. Tech. 1979)

Let us now take a brief glance at the astronomical 'drawing-board' and see whether the designs on it actually fit the facts. Let us remember that even if they did perfectly explain how the universe *might* have evolved, that would be still very far from proving that it did indeed so evolve. The Frenchman's theoretical aeroplanes, even if each one could be built and made to fly, would never disprove that the Wright Brothers came first. But the interesting thing is that not one of the theories of "cosmic evolution" does fit the facts. Prof. John Whitcomb in his 'Origin of the Solar System' has pointed out that there are at least *nine insuperable difficulties* facing the evolutionary cosmogonist. Of these we here list seven, in the form of questions:

1) If the planets were thrown off from the sun by centrifugal force, why is the sun rotating slower than any of them? An experiment with a top will soon show that small particles thown off it will lose speed much quicker than the top itself.

2) How is it that Uranus and Venus rotate (on their own axes) in the direction *opposite* to that of the other seven planets? If all nine "evolved" from the sun, it would seem inconceivable that this should be so.

31

3) How is it that 21 out of the 52 satellites of the planets revolve in a direction opposite to that of the revolution of the planets around the sun?

4) Why is it that, whereas the sun rotates much *slower* than its planets, each satellite-owning planet (except the earth) rotates *faster* than its satellites?

5) Many schoolboys are still being taught that the Moon was pulled out of the Pacific Ocean 4000 million years ago, although this theory was exploded by Harold Jeffreys in 1931. Recent research has shown that the Moon's density is only two-thirds of the Earth's. If the two bodies were originally one, why are they now so differently composed?

6) How did the earth come to have such a huge proportion of heavy elements (iron, nickel, magnesium) compared with the sun, which is 99% hydrogen and helium? Professor Hoyle says (Harper's Magazine, April 1951): "Material torn from the sun would not be at all suitable for the formation of the planets as we know them." (N.B. Here we call on Prof. Hoyle as a witness to demonstrable *facts* in the immediate *present*. This is very different from accepting his *theories* about the earth's – apart from Genesis – unknowable past and – apart from Revelation – unpredictable future.)

7) The American cosmogonist George Gamow believes that all the elements evolved out of each other by "neutron capture", beginning with hydrogen (atomic weight 1) up to the heaviest elements. Unfortunately for this theory there are two gaps in the chain: there is "no stable atom of mass 5 or mass 8. The question then is: How can the build-up of elements by neutron capture get by these gaps? The process could not go beyond helium 4, and even if it spanned this gap it would be stopped again at mass 8 ... this basic objection to Gamow's theory is a great disappointment" (quoted by Whitcomb).

In concluding this section we feel bound to draw attention to a fact hinted at before: that some scientists have a prejudice against ascribing to God any credit at all for creation. Not only do they deny that He made everything in six days: they deny that He made anything! Harlow Shapley, Emeritus Professor of Astronomy at Harvard University, makes the following remarks in 'Beyond the Observatory':

"Formerly the origin of life was held to be a matter for the Deity to take care of; it was a field for miracles and the supernatural. But no longer."

"We now believe that all the scores of kinds of atoms have evolved naturally from hydrogen, the simplest of atoms." ('Believe' is the right word to use here: it is purely a matter of faith in the unseen, because the evidence just does not exist.)

"All these (microbes, whales, sequoias, bacteria, bees, sponges) are products of the cosmic processes that evolve atoms, biological cells, plants, animals, and mankind."

The climax of Professor Shapley's New Theology is reached in these words: "To me it is a *religious* attitude to recognise the wonder of the whole natural world, not only of life ... why not *revere* also the amino acids and the simple proteins from which life emerges?" Compare this with Romans 1:21–25: "Knowing God, they have refused to honour Him as God or to render Him thanks ... they have bartered away the true God for a false one, and have offered *reverence and worship to created things* instead of to the Creator, who is blessed for ever."

Thus every theory of Cosmic Evolution so far propounded is confronted with insuperable difficulties. Even if all these were to be solved, no one could ever prove that things actually happened as they are supposed to have happened. There is no reason for doubting, but every reason for believing that God created the stars and

Solar System exactly as they are today – partly regular and partly irregular, so that man might be forced to confess: "Marvellous are Thy works ... such knowledge is too wonderful for me" (Psalm 139.14,6). This was certainly the belief of Isaac Newton, perhaps the greatest scientist of all time. And the disastrous effects of unbelief are shown by the virtual idolatry of a great astronomer.

Historical records are "scientific" in the deepest and truest sense. The historical record of God's creating the universe in six days was written by the finger of God on tables of stone, the accuracy of the whole book being vouched for by Christ Himself.

CHAPTER 7

GALILEO, DARWIN, AND 'INTERPRETATION'

"To the naked eye there is a face in the moon; it vanishes when you use a telescope. In the same way, the meanings or patterns discernible in 'history' ... disappear when we turn to history in any of the higher senses" (my italics).

C. S. Lewis, '*Historicism*'

Before proceeding further, it may be well to deal with an objection which is often raised: "Galileo was right and the Church was wrong. Therefore anyone who interprets the Bible so as to make it contradict the findings of Science is bound to be wrong, and scientific opinion is bound to be right. It's all a matter of interpretation." Let us carefully consider whether the two cases are really parallel.

1) The only words of Scripture which *seemed* to contradict Galileo were three verses (in Psalms 93:1; 96:10; 104:5), which are *poetry*. Nowhere in the historical books is there one word that denies the earth's rotation.

Darwinism, on the other hand, contradicts nearly everything written in the first eleven *chapters* of Bible *History:* it denies instant creation, the fixity of species, the special creation of man and woman, the Fall, the Curse, the universal Flood, the miraculous confusion of tongues, and the young age of the earth. All these doctrines are stated in plain prose, and many are confirmed by New Testament references.

2) Later commentators have had no difficulty in showing that the words which got Galileo into trouble ("the world is stablished that it cannot be moved") are in a sense very true. We speak of a man "keeping his place" on a football field when we mean that his position remains the same *relative to the other players*. Similarly

the earth can be said "not to move" out of its orbit and position *relative to the other planets* and the sun. This is a perfectly satisfying explanation, and has been generally accepted.

On the other hand no one has yet put forward, even after a hundred years of discussion and controversy, any acceptable harmony of Genesis and Darwinism. Somehow those 299 verses are terribly resistant to "bending"!

3) The Copernican system is *demonstrable* here and now, and explains all the phenomena. But Evolution leaves a great many phenomena unexplained; it is at best a theory "unproven and unprovable", demanding for its acceptance "faith of the highest kind: faith in the fossils which have never been found, faith in the embryonic evidence which does not exist, faith in the experiments which refuse to come off, faith unjustified by works!"

So here is the difference between Darwin and Galileo: Galileo set a demonstrable *fact* against a few words of Bible poetry which the Church at that time had understood in an obviously naive way; Darwin set an unprovable *theory* against eleven chapters of straightforward Bible history which cannot be *re*-interpreted in any satisfactory way. The 'parallel' is not parallel at all. On closer inspection the 'pattern' disappears.

This leads us on to the subject of Interpretation.

In the Bible the word 'interpret' is used only in connection with foreign languages, parables, prophecies, dreams and visions. In the Old Testament it is hardly used outside Genesis 40/41 and the book of Daniel. Two important points should be noted:

1) In every passage where things are reported contrary to natural science (sun and moon bowing down to Joseph, lean cows eating fat cows, a lion with eagle's wings), it is clearly stated that it was a dream or vision.

2) In every passage the interpretation of the dream or

36

vision is given (at least in general terms, e.g. Daniel 11). In Genesis 1–11, however, there is nothing to suggest that it is a dream or a vision or symbolic; and nowhere in the Bible do we find any interpretation of these chapters. May we not assume that from God's point of view they are *not* contrary to (super) natural science, which is the only true science of the universe? Genesis 1–11 no more requires interpretation that the statement "Balaam saddled his ass", or the cricket scores in your morning newspaper.

CHAPTER 8

IS THE EARTH "VERY GOOD" OR "CURSED"?

"Belief in words is the basis of belief in thought."

BISHOP WESTCOTT

"When I use a word, it means just what I choose it to mean."

HUMPTY DUMPTY

"If God's moral judgement differs from ours so that our 'black' may be His 'white', we can mean nothing by calling Him good."

C. S. LEWIS

The View of Older Commentators

For 18 centuries Christians took Genesis at its face value, believing that it required no more 'interpretation' than any other historical book. They accepted that the original animal world was created vegetarian (1.29,30): beasts did *not* prey upon one another, so the balance of nature must have been kept by a process which we do not now observe.

They found this view confirmed by the prophecy in Isaiah 11: "The wolf shall dwell with the lamb, and the leopard shall lie down with the kid ... the lion shall eat straw like the ox. They shall not hurt or destroy in all My holy mountain..."

Calvin comments: "Isaiah describes the order which was at the beginning before man's apostasy produced the unhappy and melancholy change under which we groan. Whence comes the cruelty of beasts ...? There would certainly have been no discord among the creatures of God, if they had remained in their original condition. When they exercise cruelty towards each other ... it is an evidence of the disorder which has sprung from the sinfulness of man ... if the stain of sin had not polluted the world, no animal would have been addicted to prey on blood, but the fruits of the earth would have sufficed for all, according to the method which God had appointed." Romans 8.19–22 seems to refer to the same event: "The creation was subjected to vanity ... the whole creation groaneth and travaileth in pain together until now."

Genesis 3.16–19 also appears to teach that, if Eve had not sinned, child-bearing would have been comparatively painless; thorns and thistles would never have existed; man would have lived without toil, on fruit plucked from trees, and the human race would have been immortal. Calvin comments: "The Lord determined that His anger should, like a deluge, overflow all parts of the earth, that wherever man might look, the atrocity of his sin should meet his eyes ... whatever unwholesome things may be produced, are not natural fruits of the earth, but are corruptions which originate from sin ... all the evils of the present life have proceeded from the same fountain. Truly the first man would have passed to a better life, had he remained upright; but there would have been no separation of the soul from the body, no corruption, no destruction, and no violent change. It is credible that woman would have brought forth without pain, if she had stood in her original condition" (Commentary, pp. 172–180).

The View of Modern Commentators

All this is flatly denied by modern Science. The dinosaurs, most ferocious of all carnivores, are supposed to have roamed the earth tearing their victims 180 million years before Man appeared. No female skeleton has ever been discovered better adapted for child-bearing than modern woman's; "prehistoric" man evidently used weapons and agricultural implements; and fossil skeletons presumably belonged to *mortal* men. So there is not one shred of tangible evidence that the Age of Innocence ever existed. Science also asserts that the ancestry of bacteria, cancer, scorpions, and other noxious creatures, can be traced back or assumed far beyond the origin of 'homo sapiens'. Which is right, Science or the Bible?

The neo-evangelical answer is that Science is right, and the older commentators were wrong in their interpretation. The all-pervading climate of Uniformitarianism has forced even reputable scholars to declare that the world *as now constituted* is "very good". Included in this "goodness" are not only thorns and thistles, cancer and leprosy, scorpions, earthquakes, childbirth without chloroform, and death, but also the rack and the thumbscrew, Sodom and Gomorrah, Belsen and the atomic bomb. "If there were no evil men, many good things would be missing in this universe" (Bernard Ramm, 'The Christian View of Science and Scripture', pp. 93–95). If irresistible logic drives Dr. Ramm to such a desperate conclusion, one may reasonably ask whether his premises are sound. For, if words can be used in the Bible with a sense opposite to that which they bear in human communications, then revelation from the mind of God to the mind of man is impossible, and the whole Christian faith is reduced to confusion. In the following chapters it will be shown that Dr. Ramm's premises (uniformitarianism, a local Flood) are *not* sound; here we shall take a closer look at the words of Scripture.

What the Bible says

Whitcomb and Morris (TGF pp. 454–473) show that the neo-evangelical view involves wresting Scripture to make it mean what no ordinary reader would ever take it to mean.

1) Romans 5 states that "by one man sin entered into the world, and *death by sin* ... death reigned *from Adam*" (not before Adam).

2) Gen. 3.18 does not say, "Cursed art *thou* from the Garden; from henceforth thou shalt be removed to the thorns and thistles"; it does say, "Cursed is *the ground* for thy sake ... thorns and thistles shall it bring forth to thee", and Gen.5.29 stresses the same fact – the Lord's curse upon *the ground*. The inescapable inference is that thorns, thistles, and all other "unwholesome things" began to grow only *after* the Fall.

3) Eve's punishment is obviously beyond the scope of scientific investigation, since *only* Eve had a perfect body, and it must have been miraculously changed to cause her and all her daughters to suffer "greatly multiplied pain" in childbirth. It is common knowledge that most animals appear to suffer far less than humans in parturition, but no evolutionist has yet explained why.

4) C. F. Keil comments on Gen.3.14:

"If these words are not to be robbed of their entire meaning, they cannot be understood in any other way than as denoting that the form and movements of the serpent were altered, and that its present repulsive shape is the effect of the curse pronounced upon it" (quoted in TGF p.465). And if God could change the shape of the serpent there is no reason to doubt that He changed the eating habits of other animals at the same time. In the Garden they were brought to Adam and were under his dominion (1.28); but after the Flood the beasts are potentially man's murderers (Gen.9.5).

Conclusion

The Age of Innocence will never be "discovered" because no *physical* record could possibly exist of a world that lasted only (perhaps) a few days or months. If a marriage breaks up after ten years, there may be nothing to show there was ever a honeymoon – nothing except the family diary. And Genesis is the first chapter in the diary of God's family. To refer to a previous illustration: in the days before photography the only possible record of Halley's Comet was *human testimony*, which was proved true when the same comet reappeared after the stated interval of years. Similarly the only possible record of the Age of Innocence is the human testimony (inspired by God) which we find in the Bible, and which will be proved true when the second Paradise appears – a kingdom in which there will again be "no more death; neither shall there be mourning, nor crying, nor pain any more ... and there shall be no more curse" (Revelation 21.4; 22.3).

All scientific and theological objections to the doctrine of the Curse are based upon (a) the idea that God *could not* have created plants and animals different from what they are now. (But if God could not do this, He is no longer God.) (b) the idea that God *does not* interfere with the course of Nature. (But this theory is contradicted throughout the Bible.) (c) denial of the universal Flood, which, as will be shown in subsequent chapters, can well account for all the fossils of dinosaurs and other flesh-eating animals: they lived and died *after* the Curse.

Surely it is more reasonable to accept the older commentators' interpretation, which Science can never disprove:

1) That the original creation was literally paradise – a perfect environment for man and woman to live in perfect health, perfect happiness, perfect holiness and fellowship with God.

2) That all our physical troubles are *not* good in the sight of God, but have been 'built-in' to "this present evil world" (Gal. 1.4) to remind us of our disobedience and continuing sinfulness. Christ healed the sick, fed the

hungry, calmed the storm and raised the dead, to demonstrate that death, storms, hunger and sickness are due simply and solely to man's sin; and that He, as Redeemer, has power to deliver not only from its penalty and pollution, but also from its effect and environment.

CHAPTER 9

THEISTIC EVOLUTION AND GENESIS 2.7

"The doctrine of Evolution, if consistently accepted, makes it impossible to believe the Bible."

T. H. HUXLEY

Many commentators and scientists today teach that "the text of Genesis would by no means disallow" (Kidner, p. 28) God's shaping man by a process of evolution. They quote as parallels Job 10.8 and Psalm 119.73: "Thine hands have made me and fashioned me." The argument runs: obviously Job and David were born in the normal way, yet they speak as if God had formed them directly. Therefore Adam too might have been born in the normal way (but of a sub-human mother), although Scripture seems to teach his direct creation from the dust of the ground (Heb. 'adamah').

However, we believe that a careful study of the text in its context will show that this interpretation is impossible, for the following reasons:

1) Job's speeches and David's psalms are not history but *poetry*. The next but one verse in Job (10.10) says:

> Hast Thou not poured me out like milk,
> And curdled me like cheese?

– which can scarcely be intended literally. In Bible exegesis almost everything depends on determining the literary genre to which a passage belongs: and we believe good reasons have been given for regarding Genesis as "sober history".

2) The Hebrew words for "living soul" in Gen.2.7 are exactly the same words as those translated "living creature" in 1.20,21,24. Therefore if Adam's body evolved from the lower animals he would have already been a "living soul/creature" long *before* God breathed into him the breath of life; and the breath of God would (on this

44

interpretation) have accomplished nothing! But Moses does not say, "God breathed into a living creature the breath of (spiritual) life, and the brute became a spiritual creature". He does say:

"God formed man (Adam) of the dust of the (inanimate) ground ('Adamah'), and breathed into his nostrils the breath of life, and man became a *living* creature." Before God breathed into him, Adam lacked one thing that the animals possessed: that is, physical life. Therefore Gen.2.7 cannot be interpreted as God's transformation of a living brute into a living man.

3) In Gen.3.19 we read: "In the sweat of thy face thou shalt eat bread, till thou return unto the ground; for out of it thou wast taken; for dust thou art, and unto dust thou shalt return."

Let us paraphrase this according to the evolutionary interpretation of Gen.2.7, and see whether it makes sense:

"... till thou return unto the sub-human brute; for out of him wast thou taken: for a sub-human brute thou art (physically), and *unto a sub-human brute thou shalt return!*" This may throw light on the doctrine of Transmigration of Souls; but more probably it highlights the impossibility of interpreting "ground" or "dust" as a metaphor for the lower animals.

4) Christ and the Apostle Paul refer to these chapters as literal historical fact:

"From the beginning of the creation (not after many millions of years) God made them male and female" (Mark 10.6).

"Woman was made out of man" (I Cor.11.12, NEB).

"For this cause (i.e. because Woman was taken out of Man) shall a man leave his father and mother, and shall cleave unto his wife" (Mat.19.5).

It is difficult to see how these verses can be reconciled with the theistic evolutionary picture of God breathing

45

His image into a pair of anthropoids. On the other hand these verses are exactly what we would expect if Christ and Paul accepted the *prima facie* interpretation of Genesis One and Two – that Eve was formed from a rib of Adam, who was formed from the ground on the Sixth Day of creation.

The Time of Man's Creation

5) Another verse very hard to reconcile with evolution is Romans 1.20: "Ever since the creation of the world (kosmos) God's invisible nature, namely, His eternal power and deity, has been clearly perceived in the things that have been made" (RSV). Bishop Handley Moule (Cambridge Bible, 'Romans', p. 60) comments: 'The Greek scarcely allows the interpretation "from the framework, or constitution, of the world". "From the creation of the world" (AV) means "since the world was created".' But how could God's power be perceived without a perceiver? Surely this implies that man must have been present *at the beginning* to praise and adore the Creator for His marvellous handiwork. The NEB is even clearer:

"Ever since the world began, God's invisible attributes have been visible to the eye of reason."

But where was the eye of reason before Man appeared? In the anthropoid ape? In the brontosaurus? In the trilobite?

If Adam was created on the Sixth Day, only two days after the sun, moon and stars, Paul's words are easily intelligible. But according to the Theory of Evolution there were no eyes of any kind to observe God's creation for the first fourteen thousand million years; animal eyes appeared only (about) five hundred million years ago; and the eye of reason (i.e. man's) only *two* million years ago. If this were true one might wonder why Paul did not write: "from the day of *man's* creation, God's power and deity have been clearly perceived, have been visible to the eye of reason" – since the whole thrust of Paul's argument is *man's* failure to glorify God. But Paul did not write this: he did write, "from the creation of the *world*" they have been visible. The simple and obvious meaning is that man's eye of reason appeared simultaneously with the rest of the 'kosmos'; that man's perception of God's invisible nature has been a fact ever since the world was completed, that is, ever since the Sixth Day.

Paul's Parallel

6) Finally, let us examine the one NT passage (I Cor. 15.40 ff.) which directly quotes Gen.2.7. Here, if anywhere, we may expect to find the true interpretation. Paul is answering the question, How are the dead raised? and with what body do they come? First he shows from Nature that there are two kinds of body – the seed and the plant; and the seed must *die* before the plant comes up. Then he continues:

"So also is the resurrection of the dead ... it is sown a natural body, it is raised a spiritual body. If there is a natural body, there is also a spiritual body. So also it is written, The first man became a living soul. The last Adam became a life-giving spirit."

Now, to what event do these last words refer? Paul is not here discussing the Incarnation, the Virgin Birth, or the human life of our Lord. He is discussing one subject only – the Resurrection. So it seems very probable that "became a life-giving spirit" refers to that moment of time in which God raised Him from the dead. Then the creation of the first Adam was exactly parallel to the resurrection of the last Adam: just as God breathed into the *lifeless* body of Christ the breath of (spiritual) life, thus making a spiritual body, so He breathed into the *lifeless* body of Adam the breath of (natural) life, thus making a natural body. The analogy is clear and striking.

Conclusion

We conclude, then, that New Testament quotations of Genesis 1–3 exclude the possibility of man's origin by theistic evolution. By all the laws of language, Gen.2.7 can only mean that Adam's body was a special creation, wholly distinct from the animals; that it was literally dead until God quickened it with natural life, just as Christ's body was literally dead until God quickened it with spiritual life. Scientifically there can never be any "explanation" of the resurrection, because the miracle will not be repeated till the return of Christ; and scientifically there can never be any explanation of man's origin, since that too was a once-for-all instantaneous miracle.

CHAPTER 10

IS GENESIS THREE A PARABLE?

"A miracle's peculiarity is that it is not interlocked with the previous history of Nature. And that is what some people find intolerable. The reason they find it intolerable is that they start by taking Nature to be the whole of reality."

C. S. LEWIS, *'Miracles'*

Many Christians are still bothered by the talking snake in Genesis 3 and try to explain it away in terms of the Book of Revelation. "If the word 'serpent' in Rev.12.9 is used symbolically, why should it not be symbolic in Genesis 3 too?" The answer lies again in a discrimination of the various types of literature found in the Bible. Revelation is a *visionary* and *symbolic* book, whereas Genesis is a *historical* book. Therefore the language used in Revelation is mostly figurative and metaphorical, while the language of Genesis is mostly straightforward and literal.

Secondly, we find that throughout Revelation, John expresses spiritual truths in terms of the historical events of the Old Testament. Seven of the plagues of Egypt (water into blood, hail, fire, sores, darkness, locusts, and frogs) are repeated; but we do not therefore conclude that the literal and physical plagues of Egypt never happened. We find "the great city which spiritually is called Sodom"; but we do not thereby infer that Lot's Sodom never existed. We find "fire and brimstone" which burn for ever, but we do not therefore deny that the Cities of the Plain were overthrown by literal fire and brimstone. In Revelation 2, 'Jezebel' and 'manna' are no doubt symbolic, but this does not mean that Ahab's wife was a disembodied spirit, or that the Israelites in the wilderness lived on thin air. Rather, every Old Testament reference in Revelation, though used spiritually in that book, confirms the historical truth of the original narrative.

God's method of teaching (as in the Tabernacle) is from the literal, visible, and tangible, to the spiritual, invisible, and intangible. So there seems to be good ground for believing that the Tree of Life in Eden was a literal botanical tree, which will have its antitype in the spiritual Tree of Life in heaven; and that the serpent in Eden was a literal zoological specimen which has its antitype in Satan. If a "dumb ass spoke with man's voice" to Balaam (as the Apostle assures us – II Peter 2.16), is it hard to believe that a dumb serpent spoke with a man's voice to Eve? Note also that when Paul refers to this event (II Cor.11.3) he says that the *serpent*, not Satan, beguiled Eve.

Another objection to the literal interpretation of Genesis 3 is based on the prophecy in v.15 – "it shall bruise thy head and thou shalt bruise his heel". These words, it is said, have a symbolic and spiritual meaning; therefore the whole passage may be symbolic and allegorical. But, once again, this inference is unwarranted, because it confuses things that differ. Even within one book of Scripture there may be several literary forms – history mingled with prophecy (e.g. Luke 3.1–6), narrative alongside parable (e.g. John 6). But this does not allow us to spiritualize the history or allegorize the narrative. So, while Genesis includes some prophecies and metaphors, especially in the utterances of God, (e.g. "the voice of thy brother's blood crieth to Me"), these can in no wise affect the literal historical truth of the narrative portions.

Finally, it has been suggested (Kidner, p. 66) that Genesis 3 is a parable like Nathan's told to David (II Sam. 12), in which David's real sin was compared to the rich man's imaginary sin. So the eating of the fruit may be only an imaginary sin representing some greater but unrecorded act of disobedience. Is this interpretation legitimate?

Every parable or allegory in Scripture *either* refers back to some historical event which has already been told in great detail (e.g. David's sin in II Sam. 11), *or* it is interpreted (e.g. Isaiah 5.7), *or* it is prophetic (e.g. Mat. 13.33), to be explained by God's working in the history of the Church. So, if Genesis 3 is a parable, it is unique: the event to which it refers is nowhere mentioned; it is not interpreted in any part of the Bible; and the story can hardly be thought of as prophetic.

Then again, all allegories and parables in both Testaments present spiritual and unfamiliar concepts in terms of natural and familiar truths. But Genesis 3 deals with things absolutely unknown to mortals – a talking snake, nakedness without shame, and life without toil. How then can we be expected to grasp a deeper spiritual truth through a story of the *un*familiar and *un*natural? This was not the method of Nathan the prophet, nor of our Lord.

In the opinion of the present writer all such non-literal interpretations, though put forward with the best of intentions in order to remove intellectual difficulties, serve only to weaken faith in the absolute power of God. Such a faith is our first and greatest requisite for the understanding of Scripture.

CHAPTER 11

BIBLICAL ARGUMENTS FOR A UNIVERSAL FLOOD

"... we may feel certain that no cataclysm has desolated the whole world. Hence we may look with some confidence to a secure future of great length."

C. DARWIN, *Origin of Species* (last page)

We now approach the most important part of our study. Whitcomb and Morris have rightly judged that all interpretation of Genesis 1–11 ultimately depends on the Flood: if it was a local inundation, then the Geological Time Scale, dinosaurs etc. cannot be fitted into any part of Scripture. On the other hand if the Flood *was* universal, it adequately explains all the phenomena; and if all the fossils were fossilized after Genesis 6, there can be no scientific or philosophical objections to the idea of a Six Day creation. 'The Genesis Flood' lists seven biblical arguments for a universal Flood:

1) *The Depth of the Flood:* the waters covered the highest mountains to a depth sufficient for the Ark to float over them. When they subsided the Ark landed on "the mountains of Ararat", of which the higher peak is 17,000 feet and the lower peak 13,000., Only after the waters had decreased for another ten weeks did the other mountain tops become visible (Gen. 8.5).

2) *The Duration of the Flood:* it prevailed for five months, and an additional seven months were required for the waters to subside and the earth to become dry. Such a flood would be quite inconceivable if limited to an area of a few hundred square miles.

3) The expression "*fountains of the great deep* were broken up" (for forty days) points unmistakably to vast

52

geological disturbances that are incompatible with the local-flood concept.

4) *The Size of the Ark:* its displacement tonnage was about 20,000 tons, and its total capacity 1,400,000 cubic feet. Not until 1884 was any bigger ship built anywhere in the world. Would such a vessel have been necessary for carrying eight passengers and a few Asiatic fauna?

5) *The Need for an Ark:* if the flood had been only local and limited, Noah and his family could easily have escaped to another country, just as Lot and his family escaped from the local and limited fire upon Sodom and Gomorrah.

6) *The Distribution of the Human Race in Noah's Day:* At least 1656 years had elapsed from the creation of Adam to the year of the Flood. Considering the longevity and fecundity of the patriarchs, there are good grounds for supposing that the population of the earth in Noah's day numbered millions, that they were widely spread, highly civilized, and possessed good communications. The hundred years while the Ark was building would have allowed plenty of time for news of Noah's preaching to reach the four corners of the world; and in order to destroy *all* flesh (mankind) the Flood would have had to cover the globe.

Evidence of human fossils in Java, China, South Africa and Western Europe, makes it difficult to assume that men did not migrate beyond the Near East before Noah's Flood.

7) *The Apostle Peter's inspired comments*: three times he refers to the destruction of the ancient *world* (kosmos). This word is used with a limited meaning only twice (Mat.4.8 – possibly; Col.1.6 – perhaps prophetically); and even if in Paul's view it meant only the Roman Empire, it is obvious that a flood which submerged the Roman Empire of 60 A.D. would have been universal.

(We must remember that it is not Noah who says that God destroyed the ancient world, but Peter; and presumably Peter's world was the same as Paul's.)

But the evidence is much stronger yet. In II Peter 3.6 the Apostle contrasts the "*kosmos* that then was" with "*the heavens and earth* that now are"; in other words 'kosmos' is the equivalent of our 'universe', comprising both heaven and earth. Peter here specifically states that the Flood destroyed (in some sense) *both* heaven *and* earth. This exacly fits the TGF hypothesis that the Flood was caused by precipitation of the water canopy surrounding the earth.

We can scarcely doubt, then, that Peter is telling us that the Flood covered the entire globe and destroyed all mankind except the Eight – just as at Christ's return the entire globe will be destroyed by fire, and only those who belong to Him will be saved.

Non-geological objections answered

Four of the commonest objections raised to the above interpretation are:

1) The words 'all' and 'every' in the Bible do not always mean literally all without exception. TGF answers this by showing, firstly, that the context of Genesis 6–9, including the tenor of the entire Flood narrative, demands a literal interpretation of the universal terms ('all' and 'every' are used 57 times in these chapters). Secondly, a flood which rose 15 cubits above Mount Ararat could not have been anything less than world-wide.

2) How could Noah have gathered and cared for all the animals, if two of *every* kind were to be included? TGF answers this by another question: How do we know that the antediluvian continents, mountains, deserts, climates and zones, were the same as ours? They were

probably quite different; and possibly all the continents were joined together by land 'bridges'. Secondly, we cannot rule out the supernatural direction of God, who said, "Two of every sort *shall come unto thee*" (6.20). Even now the word 'instinct' is used to conceal our ignorance as to how birds migrate to particular places which they have never seen. Thirdly, the size of the Ark was ample to accommodate the 35,000 vertebrate animals that would have been required. They would have fitted into 146 two-deck American stock-cars; and the Ark's capacity was 522 of these. Fourthly, it is quite probable that many of the animals "hibernated" during the year-long flood, and needed very little to eat or drink.

3) Where did the rain come from? The answer is: from the water canopy which is described in Gen.1.6–8 as "the waters which are above the firmament", and which are now mingled with the oceans. (Peter describes the antediluvian earth as "compacted out of water, and amidst water", that is, as *different* from our present earth.) So the argument that the water now present in the atmosphere would have been insufficient for the Flood, has nothing to do with the case.

4) How could the animals have reached the countries where they now live? "It is by no means unreasonable to assume that all land animals in the world today have descended from those which were in the Ark. In spite of the lack of evidence of marsupials (kangaroos etc.) having lived in Asia, it is quite conceivable that marsupials could have reached Australia by migration waves from Asia, before that continent became separated from the mainland. Comparatively little is known of the migration of animals in the past; but what we do know indicates very clearly the possibility of rapid colonization of distant areas, even though oceans had to be crossed in the process. It would not have required many centuries

for animals like the edentates (i.e. armadillos) to migrate from Asia to South America over the Bering land bridge. Population pressures, search for new homes, and especially the impelling force of God's command to the animal kingdom (Gen.8.17), soon filled every part of the habitable earth with birds, beasts, and creeping things" (TGF p.87).

Thus every one of the non-geological objections can be answered if we carefully compare the *facts* known to Science with the actual words of Scripture.

CHAPTER 12

MODERN GEOLOGY AND THE DELUGE

"We are indeed a blind race, and the next generation, blind to its own blindness, will be amazed at ours."

L. L. WHITE, quoted in A. Koestler's
'The Sleepwalkers' (1959) p. 535

At this point it will be well to remind ourselves of the use and abuse of Uniformitarianism where we have met it before. In one sense all Science depends upon it, and no one denies its validity in explaining things as they are today. For example, Halley was a Uniformitarian when he believed that a comet which had appeared at intervals of $75\frac{1}{2}$ years was probably the *same* comet, and would reappear after another $75\frac{1}{2}$ years. He was proved right by the event: the comet has a *uniform* cycle. This too is exactly what we would expect from Gen.1.14, where God says that the sun, moon and stars are for signs and seasons, days and years. Regularity of motion and appearance is the outstanding feature of the heavenly bodies.

On the other hand we perceived that Uniformitarianism breaks down completely in the face of miracles, which are *not* day-to-day (or century-to-century) occurrences, but occasional and special acts of God. It is therefore impossible to explain creation on the basis of Uniformitarianism, because creation was unique and unrepeatable ("the heaven and the earth were *finished*, and all the host of them. And on the seventh day God *finished* his work which He had made"). It will now be shown that Uniformitarianism also fails to explain the phenomena connected with the Flood, because this event too has been declared by God to be unique and unrepea-

57

table: "Neither will I again smite any more every living thing, as I have done" (Gen.8.21).

The Inadequacy of Uniformitarianism

This doctrine has been well explained by R. W. Fairbridge, Professor of Geology at Columbia University (quoted in TGF, p. 131): "In their effort to establish natural causes for the grand-scale workings of nature, 19th century geologists spurned the Scriptural concept of catastrophe. Under the leadership of the Scottish pioneers, James Hutton and Charles Lyell, they advanced the principles of uniformitarianism, which held that *the events of the past could be explained in the light of processes at work in the present*" (our italics). But TGF points out that this principle is quite inadequate to explain the following:

1) Volcanism and Igneous Rocks

Millions of square miles of these, thousands of feet deep, are found all over the world (e.g. the Deccan Plateau of India). No volcano ever known to man has produced anything like this quantity of lava; so it must have been produced by a process *not* repeated and *not* observed today.

2) Mountains

"All the major mountain ranges evidently were uplifted within the most recent eras of geologic history", yet "geologists are still unable to agree on a satisfactory hypothesis of mountain-building". Why is the earth not perfectly smooth all round? Why are mountains not coming up every day? Nobody knows. The past *cannot* be explained in the light of processes at work in the present.

3) Continental Ice Sheets

According to some geologists, four million square miles of North America and two million square miles of Europe were once glaciated. At least 29 'explanations' of this have been put forward, but every one has been found untenable in the light of further information. And we do not observe continental ice-sheets forming today.

4) Sedimentation

The argument here is highly technical, but we quote one example: most of Utah and Arizona, with large segments of Colorado and New Mexico – in all some 250,000 square miles of plateau – have been uplifted from far below sea-level (since most of its sediments are of marine origin) to over a mile above sea-level, without at all disturbing the flatness of the strata! Such an uplift is quite unparalleled in historic times, and quite inexplicable in terms of uniformity. "By far the most reasonable way of accounting for the Grand Canyon is in terms of rapid deposition out of the sediment-laden water of the Flood" (TGF p. 153).

5) Fossil Graveyards

How and why were the five million mammoths of Siberia frozen to death in solid ice? How is it that in the water-laid "bone-bed" at Agate Springs, Nebraska, fossils are found of the rhinoceros, camel, giant boar, and numerous other animals not indigenous to America? How is it that in the Baltic amber deposits modern insects are found belonging to all regions of the earth? How could 800,000 million skeletons of vertebrate animals be entombed together in the Karroo formation (South Africa)? To account for these phenomenal mass-burials, and many more like them, in terms of present-day processes is absolutely impossible.

59

6) Coal beds

"Regardless of the exact manner in which coal was formed, it is quite certain that there is nothing corresponding to it taking place in the world today" (TGF p. 165).

7) Footprints of extinct animals

(A photograph of dinosaur tracks is shown.) "It seems clear that the only way in which such prints could be preserved as fossils is by means of some chemical action permitting rapid lithification and some aqueous action permitting rapid burial. Sudden and catastrophic action is necessary for any reasonable explanation of the phenomena" (TGF p. 168).

8) Living Fossils

Palaeontology is quite unable to account for the survival of some creatures which were supposed to have become extinct aeons ago. Among these the tuatara, a New Zealand reptile, has no ancestors after 135 million B.C.; the coelecanth, a deep-sea fish, has no ancestors after 70 million B.C., and a mollusc named 'neopilina galathea' has no ancestors after 280 million B.C.! How then did they leap the huge gap in the rocks? (If we believe the Bible, all is explained: some of their ancestors were fossilized in the Flood, but some survived. The Tuatara's ancestors presumably got a seat in the Ark.)

9) Rock Formations out of sequence

This evidence of itself is fatal to the theory of fossils being deposited at a uniform slow rate all over the earth, by "ages". This theory was framed by men who presumed (without proof) that any rock in which a "lower" creature is found must have been physically lower than any rock in which a "higher" creature is found; but the theory is contradicted by the facts over thousands of miles of the earth's surface. The "older" rocks are on top, and the "younger" rocks are below; and to account for this the "older" rocks are supposed to have been pushed into place by some enormous (but inexplicable) "overthrust" from miles away. In TGF many impressive examples are given, e.g. in the Mythen Peak of the Alps, Eocene rocks (supposedly 60 million years old) are found under Triassic (supposedly 200 million years old). To account for this the Triassic rock, plus the Jurassic and Cretaceous above it, is said to have been pushed all the way from Africa to Switzerland!

Conclusion

We conclude this chapter with a quotation from Dr. E. M. Spieker, Professor of Geology at Ohio State University (TGF p. 209): "Does our time scale, then, partake of natural law? No ... I wonder how many of us realize that the time scale was frozen in essentially its present form by 1840? How much world geology was known in 1840? A bit of western Europe, none too well, and a lesser fringe of eastern North America. All of Asia, Africa, South America, and most of North America, were virtually unknown. How dared the pioneers assume that their scale would fit the rocks in these vast areas, by far the major part of the world? Only in dogmatic assumption ... and in many parts of the world, notably in India and South America, it does not fit. But even there it is applied! The followers of the founding fathers went forth across the earth and in Procrustean fashion made the scale fit the sections they found, even in places where the actual evidence proclaimed denial. So flexible and accommodating are the "facts" of geology" (1956).

CHAPTER 13

CATASTROPHE COVERS IT ALL

"Lyell is firmly convinced that he has shaken people's faith in the Deluge far more efficiently by never having said a word against the Bible."

From the Letters of Charles Darwin

All that now remains is to show positively that the Flood described in the Bible could have and would have been sufficient to cause all the geological effects which we have mentioned. (In TGF many effects are listed which we have *not* mentioned: most of them will be of interest to specialists only.)

1) Volcanism, Igneous Rocks, and Mountains
In Genesis 7.11 we read, "All the fountains of the great deep were broken up": this would probably include vast submarine eruptions, and the uplifting of the world's major mountain ranges. "Oozing lava built great plateaus which now cover 200,000 square miles in Washington, Oregon, Idaho, and northern California. An even larger eruption created India's famous Deccan Plateau, whose once molten rock extends two miles below the surface" (TGF p. 127). The discovery of fossil fish high up in the Alps and other ranges strongly suggests that they were uplifted at this time.

2) Continental Ice Sheets
If these did in fact occur, they may have been formed (a) by the sudden change of weather caused by precipitation of the water canopy (which had acted as a 'greenhouse', keeping the earth warm), or (b) by the upheaval of mountain chains with their snow-caps, or (c) by the great accumulation of ice near the Poles.

3) Coal Beds

As everyone knows, these were formed by enormous quantities of dead vegetation being subjected to heavy pressure. It is not so well known that the coal did not sink down 'in situ', but was *water*-laid. Dr. Heribert-Nilson writes that only a process of immense magnitude and world-wide effect could account for the coal seams. More recently (1972) Dr. George R. Hill of the College of Mines and Mineral Industries, University of Utah, has demonstrated the rapid formation of coal from wood or other cellulosic material. He writes: "These observations suggest that in their formation high rank coals were probably subjected to high temperature at some stage in their history. A possible mechanism ... could have been a short time, rapid heating event".[1]

[1] Chem Tech, May 1972 p. 296, quoted in 'The World That Perished' p. 83.

4) Fossils

(a) The Siberian mammoths may well have been overwhelmed when the 'canopy' was precipitated and the resulting floods of water froze at the Poles. The suggestion that the earth's axis was tilted out of the perpendicular at this time was first made by Edmund Halley and would seem quite credible since it is *after* the Flood that cold and heat, summer and winter, are first mentioned (Gen. 8.22). (b) The animal graveyards are what one would expect in a universal deluge: millions of fish were smothered by mud, and mammals of all kinds huddled together in caves to escape the rising waters. The disappearance of the rhinoceros from America is easily accounted for by the Flood, but hard to explain otherwise. (c) The *general order* of deposition of the fossils, too, is easily accounted for: at the bottom would be shellfish (the heaviest), then vertebrate fish, then amphibians, land reptiles, birds and mammals. The larger and more mobile animals would have been able to keep out of the Flood longer than the smaller and less mobile. But on the other hand the currents must have ebbed and flowed with tremendous force, scouring, uprooting, over-turning and returning many times before they eventually subsided. This explains the frequent *dis*order of fossils in the sedimentary rocks: sometimes the dead trolobites got swept on top of the dead pterodactyls. (d) *Dinosaurs.* Many people are puzzled by the existence of these creatures, which do not appear to be mentioned in the Bible. Why were they created? Were they represented in the Ark? Why are they now extinct? Our answers can be only tentative.

It is possible that they are mentioned in Gen.1.21 ("great sea-monsters", RV), though this would seem to include only the amphibians. Of course there is nothing to exclude them from "the beasts of the earth" (Gen. 1.25). They might have been herbivorous before the Curse; or they might have been sent as a punishment for man's sin of violence (Gen. 6.11), as God threatened to do to His people in later history (Dt. 32.24 – "I will also send the teeth of beasts upon them". These beasts would be ordinary mammals, presumably). There may have been young dinosaurs aboard the Ark; and these may have been killed off by the post-diluvial climate. That they were once contemporary with man is suggested by the ancient and widespread belief in *dragons*. Even the Encyclopaedia Britannica (14th ed.) allows that primitive peoples may have derived the idea from dinosaur bones; but it seems more probable that Noah's sons had seen live dinosaurs, and passed them on to their posterity in the form of pictures.

For the present argument it is sufficient to know that the dinosaurs whose fossil remains we possess almost certainly died by *drowning*. The Dinosaur National Monument in Utah and Colorado is one of several huge graveyards found in various parts of the world. One writer describes it in these terms: "A majority of the remains of 300 dinosaurs probably floated down an eastward-flowing river until they were stranded on a sandbar. Perhaps the stegosaurs drowned trying to ford a tributary stream, or were washed down during floods ..." TGF comments: "One could hardly ask for a better description of the way in which these great reptiles were overwhelmed, drowned and buried by the Deluge waters."

5) Sedimentation

It is generally admitted that almost all the sedimentary rocks of the earth, which are the ones containing fossils, have been laid down by moving waters. The O.E.D. defines sediment as "earth or detrital matter deposited by aqueous agency". Obviously these great masses of sediment must have been first eroded, then transported, then deposited – "exactly the sort of thing that occurs in any flood, and which must have occurred on a uniquely grand scale during the great Flood of Genesis".

6) Submarine geology

Submarine geology confirms the concept of a universal Flood. Since 1950 large numbers of "drowned islands" have been discovered – many of them more than 6000 feet below the surface, yet bearing abundant evidence that they were once above it! Also submarine canyons, hundreds of miles long, are very difficult to explain in terms of the present ocean level. Dr. K. K. Landes, Chairman of the Department of Geology at the University of Michigan, writes: "Can we, as seekers after truth, shut our eyes any longer to the fact that large areas of sea floor have sunk vertical distances measured in miles?" (TGF p. 412). Uniformitarianism cannot account for this: but on the hypothesis of a Deluge precipitated from the upper atmosphere, all is explained. Before the Flood there was much less sea in proportion to land, and the land was much flatter. When the rain rained, first of all the earth was covered to a great depth; then volcanism and 'tectonic' activity built up the mountains; simultaneously the deep ocean beds sank down to accommodate the vastly increased waters on the surface of the globe. Thus the islands were "drowned", and the river canyons became submarine canyons. It is probably to this event that the Psalmist (104) refers:

"The waters stood above the mountains.

At Thy rebuke they fled;

At the voice of Thy thunder they hasted away

(The mountans rose, the valleys sank down)

Unto the place which Thou hadst founded for them."

7) The Antediluvian Climate

Finally, the *Antediluvian Climate* powerfully confirms the concept of a universal Flood. In spite of the millions of years supposedly separating trilobites from dinosaurs, and dinosaurs from mammals, it is firmly established that the climate of nearly *all* "ages" was warm and mild over the whole earth. For instance "in the Eocene age (60 million B.C.) subtropical heat was experienced in Greenland" (TGF p. 244). Uniformitarian geologists are at a loss to explain this tremendous difference from things as we see them today: they are forced to conclude that it must be due to changes in solar radiation. But Professor Hoyle states: "There is no evidence that changes take place in the radiation of the sun" (TGF p. 253).

On the other hand one of the most original and convincing arguments of TGF concerns the 'canopy' already mentioned, for which the Bible phrase is 'the waters above the firmament' (Gen. 1.7). They were invisible, held in suspension in the form of water vapour; and *they* caused the universally warm climate by trapping the sun's rays like a greenhouse. This accounts for the absence of rain before the Flood (Gen. 2.5), and the absence of clouds and rainbows too (Gen. 9.13 seems to imply this). Above all, it accounts for the Deluge: at God's command the vapour precipitated millions of tons of water, which first overflowed the earth, then drained off into the newly formed ocean beds. Only *after* this did the 'normal' hydrologic cycle – evaporation, clouds, and rain – begin. This seems to be a thoroughly satisfying solution to the problem.

CHAPTER 14

ARCHAEOLOGICAL DATING

"Why have no poets sung of feats before the Theban war and the tragedy of Troy? The answer is, I believe, that this world is newly-made: its origin is a recent event, not one of remote antiquity. That is why even now some arts are still being perfected ...."

LUCRETIUS (Roman philosopher),
ON THE NATURE OF THINGS, 60 BC

The 'vapour canopy' seems also to be the answer to another question that is often asked: Has not Carbon 14 dating proved that the history of Man goes back much farther than 4000 B.C.?

TGF thoroughly discusses this and other chemical dating methods (pp. 332–378), and the conclusion is that they all presuppose the *uniformity of the present atmosphere with the past*. "Carbon 14 dating assumes that the amount of C^{14} in the air has remained constant throughout the ages, but there is no proof, independent of the method itself, that cosmic-ray intensity has remained constant". Similarly Professor Wilder Smith expounds at length the "built-in potential errors" of C^{14} dating (pp. 116–126); and Professor W. F. Libby of California, who invented C^{14} dating, in 1946, has admitted: "It is noteworthy that the earliest astronomical fix is at 4000 years ago, that all older dates have errors, and that these are more or less cumulative with time before 4000 years ago" ('Science', April 19, 1963). The National Geographic Society News Bulletin for June, 1961, carried this statement: "Analyses of iron in ancient bricks indicate that the magnetism may have declined by about two-thirds over the past 2000 years ... Carbon 14 results from the collision of cosmic rays with nitrogen atoms in the air. If the amount of Carbon 14 has varied due to changes in the magnetic field, and has not remained a reliable constant for measuring age, *many estimates may be in error*." (our italics)

TGF mentions another very interesting fact: that the oldest trees in the world, the giant sequoias and bristlecone pines of California, are apparently the *first* generation, since no one has discovered any old stumps of dead ones. Some of these trees are more than 4000 years old; but the question is, Why are there none older? – since they appear to be immune to pests and disease. A probable answer is that their ancestors were wiped out by the Flood 40 to 45 centuries ago.

Can we trust the textbooks?

Christians who read books on Archaeology would be well advised to take all the dates prior to 2000 B.C. with a large pinch of salt. Nearly all modern archaeologists entirely discount the Flood, and base their figures on one or more of these: (a) Carbon 14 dating (b) layers of 'culture' dug up on ancient sites (c) ancient records of doubtful accuracy (d) uniformitarian presuppositions. That all of these are very uncertain, and admit of no truly scientific proof, can be seen from the following examples:

(a) "Dr. Stuart Piggott, a British archaeologist, reports that two radio-carbon tests on a sample of charcoal indicated a date of 2620–2630 B.C. for an ancient structure at Durrington Walls in England. But absolutely compelling archaeological evidence called for a date approximately 1000 years later" (TGF p. 43).

(b) In "the world's oldest city", The Jericho Tower now dated 6850 B.C. was dated 4800 B.C. in 1955 when Dr. Ehrich's book 'Relative Chronologies in Old World Archaeology' was published. In the 1929 edition of the Encyclopaedia Britannica the date of the Great Pyramid was B.C. 4800. When the present writer was at school in 1938 he was assured that the correct date is B.C. 3800. Today the date has dropped to B.C. 2580. These varying opinions would seem to indicate that archaeological dating is still somewhat less than an exact science.

(c) The dates of the kings of Egypt are based chiefly on the writings of Manetho, a Greek priest (c. 285 B.C.). But one version of his list presents us with 561 kings who reigned 5524 years, whereas another version lists 361 kings who reigned 4480 or 4780 years. Further, many of the dynasties may have reigned at the same time in different parts of Egypt. Alexander Hislop ('The Two Babylons', 4th ed. 1953, App. B) wrote: "Bunsen casts overboard all Scripture chronology and sets up the unsupported dynasties of Manetho as if they were sufficient to override the Divine word as to a question of historical fact. But if the Scriptures are not historically true, we can have no assurance of their truth at all. It is worthy of note that though Herodotus vouches for the fact that there were no fewer than twelve contemporaneous kings in Egypt, Manetho has made no allusion to this, but has made his Thinite, Memphite, and Diospolitan dynasties of kings, and a long etcetera of other dynasties, all successive!" Manetho also lists the 'Reign of the Gods' lasting 13,900 years. That his work has some value is not denied, but it cannot be compared with the Bible for trustworthiness. Martin Anstey (1913, 'Romance of Bible Chronology', p. 94) writes: "The Egyptians themselves never had any chronology at all. They were devoid of the chronological idea."

(d) Dr. Paul Thieme, Professor of Sanskrit and Comparative Philology at Yale University, writes as follows:

"Indo-European, I conjecture, was spoken on the Baltic coast of Germany late in the fourth millennium B.C. (i.e. about 3200). Since our oldest documents of

Indo-European daughter languages (in Asia Minor and India) date from the second millennium B.C., the end of the fourth millennium would be a likely time anyhow. 1000 or 1500 years are a time sufficiently long for the development of the changes that distinguish our oldest Sanskrit speech from what we construct as Indo-European" (quoted in TGF p. 395).

But this theory allows no place for the Tower of Babel and the confusion of tongues, which (according to Moses, Gen.11.7) was effected instantaneously and did *not* evolve over many centuries. (We do not, of course, deny that there has been development *since* the miracle at Babel.) Like Professor Gamow's speculation as to the origin of the universe and solar system, Professor Thieme's "conjecture" about the origin of Sanskrit is squarely based on uniformitarian presuppositions unsupported by any historical evidence whatever.

CHAPTER 15

THE ORIGIN OF LANGUAGE

"Noam Chomsky's view is that language is programmed into human beings. There is absolutely no evidence that it evolved."

MICHAEL PITMAN, *Adam & Evolution (1984)*

The phenomenon of language appears to present an impassable stumbling-block to the theory of man's evolution. In their first flush of enthusiasm some Darwinians attempted "to prove from the anatomical structure of the skulls of the earliest prehistoric men that they could not have possessed the faculty of speech ... but this conclusion is certainly drawn from insufficient premises, and has no foundation in fact" (Enc. Brit. 14th ed. article 'Language'). Assuming that the first men could *not* talk, evolutionists put forward various theories of the origin of language. The best known of these are the bow-wow, pooh-pooh, and yo-he-ho theories. Men are supposed to have imitated animal sounds (bow-wow) or uttered instinctive emotional cries (pooh-pooh) or natural singsong at team-work (yo-he-ho: the Volga boatmen). This, according to 19th century experts, was the beginning of speech. Obviously, then, the more primitive a language, the more monosyllabic it should be.

But modern research among the 'primitive' peoples of the world has proved these ideas to be pure fantasy. Dr. Eugene Nida writes in 'Customs and Culture (1954, p. 205):

"During the last century there was a popular evolutionary belief that languages had evolved from monosyllabic structure (such as Chinese) through the agglutinative structure of such languages as Bantu and Aztec to 'the highest form of speech', the inflected languages of

Europe. Such blatant egoism has been found lacking any basis in fact. Even Chinese, which was cited as such a primitive language, was discovered to have had some inflection in its earlier history. As for 'primitive languages', they have been shown to exhibit all the types of structure found in any language spoken by 'civilized' peoples ... languages are arbitrary systems: there is nothing in the nature of the sounds themselves which makes it obligatory for them to carry particular meanings ..... even exclamations show no basic similarities. We yell "Ouch!", but a Spanish-speaking person cries "Ay! Ay!" Our dogs bark bow-wow, but the Kipsigis of Kenya insist that dogs say 'u 'u. It is entirely arbitrary as to which sounds are to be employed to represent particular ideas or emotional responses."

Earlier Dr. Nida states that "there is no tribe of people anywhere in the world which does not have thousands of words in its vocabulary, and an intricate systematic way of putting words together into phrases and sentences, i.e. a grammar." The Yaagans of Tierra del Fuego – a nomadic tribe – have a vocabulary of 30,000 words, as do the Zulus of South Africa. "Almost any verb root in Aymara (Peru) can occur in at least 100,000 different combinations." Some Bantu languages have a grammar more rigid and precise than Greek: "each word must come in a specific order and begin with a prefix which indicates the system of modification ... Wintu Indians of California have special forms which indicate whether a statement is (1) hearsay (2) a result of direct observation, or (3) inferred, with three degrees of plausibility."

Among the great scholars of the Victorian era, few if any excelled Richard Chenevix Trench as a philologist. From a study of world-wide Missions he concluded that language is not an art (like tool-making) but an instinct or God-given faculty, like the bee's instinct to make cells and the bird's to make its nest. Why? Because there are

73

tribes which use no tools and cannot even cook; but "there have never yet been found human beings who do not employ speech." Secondly he maintains that "the theory that the savage was the seed out of which in due time civilized man was unfolded ... is contradicted by every notice of our actual experience. Here, as in everything else that concerns the great original institutes of humanity, our best and truest lights are to be gotten from a study of the first three chapters of Genesis. What does the language of primitive savages on close inspection prove to be? In every case it is the remnant and the ruin of a better and nobler past ... as one habit of civilization after another has been let go, the words which those habits demanded have dropped as well, first out of use then out of memory." The Bechuanas of South Africa at one time used the word 'Morimo' to mean 'Him that is in Heaven', a supreme Divine Being. But Moffat (1840) found that the word and the idea had almost vanished from the Bechuana vocabulary of his day. "Here and there he could meet with an old man, scarcely one or two in a thousand, who remembered in his youth to have heard speak of 'Morimo' (Trench, 'On the Study of Words' pp. 12–16). This example shows that there is nothing 'automatic' about a language improving or expanding. When the Bantu invaded South Africa they may have had a much richer vocabulary than at present.

Ancient Languages

What about ancient languages? If Evolution be true, will not the oldest be the simplest?

Everyone knows that Latin is much harder than English – cases, genders, moods, voices, personal terminations and precise syntax. Greek, perhaps 600 years older than Latin, is still more difficult; and when we come to Vedic Sanskrit (c. 1500 B.C.) the complexity is almost

74

unbelievable. The article in the Encyclopaedia Britannica reads: "In the Vedic language the verbal system is of considerable complexity. A verb might have various stems, viz. present (sometimes more than one), aorist (three), perfect (characterized by reduplication and peculiar terminations), future. The various present stems indicated various types of present-stem action, such as intensive, repetitive, inchoative, causative, desiderative etc. Each of the first three stems had five moods – indicative expressing fact, injunctive and subjunctive expressing will and futurity, optative and imperative. In the indicative of the present, perfect and future stems there were two tenses, present and past ... each tense had three persons and three numbers – singular, dual and plural. Finally, each tense could be conjugated in two voices with different terminations – active and middle. Among the parts of the infinitive verb there was connected with each stem a participle which could be either active or middle, and independent of tense stems a past principle, one or more infinitives, a gerundive and an indeclinable participle or gerund. The total number of possible forms belonging to any one verb is thus very great ... this verbal system was *greatly simplified in Classical Sanskrit* (500 B.C.–1000 A.D.)". (our italics)

Modern English

Coming down to modern English, in which most verbs have less than a dozen possible forms (e.g. do, dost, does, did, didst, done, doing), we realize that we are at the end of a long line of *devolution*. So far from being the highly complex descendant of a simple non-grammatical ancestor, our speech is the simple, (comparatively) monosyllabic, (comparatively) non-grammatical descendant of a highly-inflected, complex, polysyllabic and exactly grammatical ancestor!

We conclude, then, that in language the natural direction is *down*, from the higher and more difficult to the lower and easier. Nowhere on the face of the earth is there evidence of evolution from simple to complex: everywhere the evidence points to devolution from complex to simple.

Unrelated Languages

A second very interesting fact discovered by modern research is that there are at least 50 distinct families of languages. Nine of them include nearly 90% of the world's population – Indo-European, Sino-Tibetan, Semitic-Hamitic, Dravidian, Ural-Altaic, Japanese, Malayo-Polynesia, Bantu, and Austroasiatic; and the remaining 40 odd are spoken by comparatively small groups, e.g. the Basques of the Pyrenees, whose language cannot be related to any other in Europe (Nida, p. 103). Between these families there is no evidence of any common source or historical connection (although there are linguists who believe that such a connection will one day be proved, and still search for it). Japanese, for example, is totally different from Arabic, and both are totally different from Bantu. Yet almost all anthropologists now admit the unity of the human race. Why then are our languages so distinct? If we rule out the theory of random evolution from monosyllables, for which there is no evidence whatever, there seems to be only one possible answer: the story of the Tower of Babel in Genesis 11 is literally and historically true.

Speech was God's gift to man at his creation: Adam was able to understand verbal commands, to name the animals, to name his wife (*not* at random, but meaningfully), to talk with her, and with God. Till a hundred years after the Flood, it seems, "the whole earth was of one language and one speech". Most commentators take this to mean that they used the same vocabulary and the same pronunciation. Then God did a miracle of judgement, instantly confounding their language so that they might not understand one another. Hence Japanese, Arabic, Bantu etc. It is true that an Englishman, a Frenchman and a German who knew not one word of each other's language would be equally at a loss to understand each other; but the actual evidence suggests that God not merely split up one language family into many related branches, but initiated many perfectly distinct methods of verbal communication. Every one of these languages, we may presume, was highly complex, and included a large vocabulary. Over the course of centuries some fortunate tribes (like the Greeks) learned to write, and produced a brilliant literature. Others got lost in the jungle. But even the most 'primitive' tribes still retain in their language a relic of the glorious past, a proof that they are cousins of those who built the Pyramids, and of those who fought at Troy.

Conclusion

We conclude, then, that as astronomers have failed to explain the origin of the solar system in terms of cosmic evolution, as geologists have failed to explain the origin of mountains and 'drowned' islands, as biologists have failed to explain the Origin of Species – let alone of Man; so archaeologists, anthropologists and linguists have completely failed to explain the origin of Language in terms of naturalism, uniformitarianism and evolution. Once again the Bible supplies us with the only explanation perfectly congruous with all the known *facts*.

CHAPTER 16

WHERE HAS SCIENCE GONE WRONG?

"The idols of the theatre are the authoritative opinions of others which a man likes to accept as a guide when interpreting something he hasn't experienced himself ...
"Another idol of the theatre is our over-willingness to agree with the arguments of science. One can sum this up as the voluntary acceptance of other people's errors!"
"That's good," said Oleg ... "Voluntary acceptance of other people's errors! That's it!"

'Cancer Ward', Alexander Solzhenitsyn

Two questions remain to be answered:

1) If all these facts are so, why do most modern scientists reject the Bible account of the Flood and cling to the Geological Time Scale? We believe the answer is found in the Bible itself:

"In the last days there will come men who will say, Where is now the promise of His (Christ's) coming? Our fathers have been laid to their rest, but still everything continues exactly as it has always been since the world began." (Uniformitarianism!) "In taking this view they *deliberately ignore* (or wilfully forget) the fact that by water the first world was destroyed, the water of the Deluge" (II Peter 3.3–7). God has set His unmistakable mark upon the earth. The destruction of billions of His own creatures, the burial of trillions of tons of vegetation, the depression of old continents and the uplifting of new ones – these mighty acts proclaim the power and holiness of our Creator. But the geologists, biologists and archaeologists (like some astronomers) "glorified Him not as God, neither were thankful, but became vain in their imaginations". *This* accounts for their misconstruing the evidence and turning it against God's Word.

Only in the last two centuries have scientists come to doubt the reality of the universal Flood, and Peter tells us this is a sign of the *last* days before the coming of Christ.

2) If all these facts are so, why do many sincere Christians believe that the universe is millions of years old, and that the Flood was only a local event?

Perhaps these sincere Christians have been "carried away with the error of the wicked", because the particular error against which St. Peter here[1] warns us is the misinterpretation of Scripture. St. Paul wrote to sincere Christians in Colosse about the dangers of "philosophy and vain deceit", and to sincere Christians in Ephesus about the "sleight of men, craftiness and error". Church History shows that sincere Christians have often erred from the truth. There have been other periods when all Western civilization was the victim of a gigantic hoax, when millions of people were persuaded to abandon God's truth in the Bible and embrace "hollow and delusive speculations based on traditions of man-made teaching".

Gnosticism

Our first example is the Gnostic heresy. When St. Paul warned Timothy against "oppositions of *science* falsely so called", he used the word 'gnosis'. Professor F. F. Bruce has written: "The general name given to the new learning was *gnosis*. This is simply the Greek word for knowledge, but it tended to be used in a superior sense, much in the same way that more recently the Latin word for knowledge, *scientia* or science, has come to be spelt with a capital letter and used almost personally as the subject of sentences. "Science tells us" that such and such is the case; that was very much the way in which people of those days spoke of *gnosis*. When Christianity made

79

headway in the Greek world, it soon came into collision with the possessors of *gnosis*, who were Gnostics (the people who possess real knowledge). The result was an attempt *to restate Christianity in terms of gnosis, to fit it into the current cosmology*". (our italics)

Now it would not be unfair to say that most commentaries on Genesis since 1870 are exactly this – attempts to restate the Bible doctrines of Creation, the Fall, and the Curse, in terms of the current cosmology – "the assured results of Science".

Prof. Bruce continues: "The new theosophy was very attractive, and throughout the second century it made considerable headway among the more intellectual Christians of the Graeco-Roman world. While it was pre-Christian in origin, deriving elements from pagan thought, and absorbing a good deal of sheer magic in the process, it developed a variety of definitely Christianized forms." And the Enc. Brit. states: "one of the determining forces of Gnosticism was a *fantastic oriental imagination*."

We may confidently predict that in ages to come other historians will write somewhat as follows (with apologies to F. F. Bruce): "The new Scientism was very attractive, and throughout the 19th and 20th centuries it made considerable headway among the more intellectual Christians of the Western world. While it was pre-Christian in origin, deriving elements from pagan thought, it developed a variety of definitely Christianized forms (e.g. Theistic Evolution). However, it was finally exposed as nothing but another "hollow and delusive speculation" of men who totally misconstrued the evidence deposited by the Noahic Deluge. Christians at last awoke to the fact that all the fossils could be explained in terms of the Flood, and that one of the determining forces of Scientism was a *fantastic occidental imagination* which could explain every irregularity in the solar system without explanation, leap the gaps in the atomic series without evidence (by "sheer magic"), postulate the discovery of fossils which have never been discovered, and prophesy the success of breeding experiments which have never succeeded. Of this kind of science it might truly be said that it was 'knowledge falsely so called'!"

Mediaeval Superstition

"In their greed for money they will trade on your credulity with sheer fabrications."
II Peter 2.3, NEB

Another astonishing example of credulity is the mediaeval belief in Relics. Starting as veneration for the martyrs in the 2nd and 3rd centuries, this grew into a reverence for anything supposed to have had some connection with the saints or the Saviour. Frauds, pious and impious, flooded the market. At the cathedral of Trier the seamless robe of Christ was "discovered" early in the 12th century; the bodies of the "three kings" (who saw the Star) were deposited at Cologne in 1164 by Frederick I; at least two French churches possessed "the crown of thorns"; King Athelstan (930 A.D.) donated to the monastery at Exeter fragments of "the candle which the angel of the Lord lit in the tomb of Christ, of the Burning Bush, and of one of the stones which slew Stephen". In 1520 Frederick the Wise, Luther's protector, had 19,013 such relics in the Schlossekirche at Wittenberg. Thus thousands of sincere and intelligent Christians over hundreds of years were completely deceived, not only as to the spiritual efficacy of these relics, but also as to their *history*, which of course had no connection with the acts or facts of the Bible.

Let no one think that the human race is less gullible today than 700 or 1700 years ago: the gullibility has changed not in degree but in direction. As C. S. Lewis wrote in 'Screwtape Letters', the devil uses fashions in thought to distract men from their real dangers. In an age of magic and 'miracles', faith can quickly degenerate into superstition; and in a sceptical anti-superstitious age men can easily be persuaded that "miracles don't happen", that only Science is infallible, that whatever the "experts" say must be true even when there is no evidence whatever to support their statements. Today these unproven statements are held in the same naive veneration as were the relics of the Middle Ages.

Modern Scientism

"When men cease to believe in God, they do not believe in nothing, they believe in anything." G. K. CHESTERTON

Two final examples will show the cul-de-sac into which Evolution has led its devotees.

1) As everyone knows, some marine creatures are not fish but mammals: over 100 species of whale (including dolphins and porpoises); the dugong of the Indian Ocean, and the manatee of tropical American and African waters; and 47 species of seal (including sea-lions, fur-seals, true seals, sea-elephants, and walruses) numbering about 25 million – "the largest surviving group of big carnivorous animals in the world today" ('Life' Nature Library, 'The Sea'). Evolutionists confidently affirm that all these were once land animals which one day took a walk into the sea (their fishy ancestors having crawled *out* of the sea in order to become land animals) and by a process of gradual adaptation were transformed into the highly efficient swimmers and divers which we now see. A land mammal could not, of course, become a whale overnight. It is estimated that at least thirty intermediate forms would have been necessary. But what is *not* stated in the evolutionary textbooks is this: that

among all the thousands of fossils which have been examined, *not one has ever been discovered* which could begin to bridge the gap; not one half-whale, half-walrus or half-seal; not one "link" which might be part of the chain connecting land animals with "the largest group of big carnivorous animals in the world today"! And it was T. H. Huxley who wrote:

"The primary and direct evidence in favour of evolution can be furnished *only* by palaeontology (fossil remains) ... if evolution has taken place, there will its mark be left: if it has not taken place, there will be its refutation."

2) The same can be said of another mammal which apparently got bored with its natural environment and found no difficulty in constructing for itself the most efficient flying machine ever invented, plus built-in radar. We refer, of course, to the Bat, whose marvellous dexterity in flight has been proved to excel any bird's. There are several hundred species of them, inhabiting most parts of the globe, and numbering many millions. Once again the evolutionist is forced to postulate intermediate stages for the development of a ground-mammal into an air-mammal: in this case they reckon the figure is twenty. But once again the links are missing: not a single fossil has ever been discovered of *any* creature which can be called a "half-bat", let alone twenty distinct stages. Science has accepted the dogma of the bat's evolution in spite of a *total lack of palaeontological evidence.*

If we pause a moment to enquire whether there is any connection between the mediaeval belief in Relics and the modern belief in Evolution, we shall find that both delusions stem from a common principle of *transferred authority.* People accepted the authenticity and efficacy of relics because the Church which guaranteed them was founded upon truth: the life, death and resurrection of

Jesus Christ, and the New Testament. These truths commended themselves to the conscience of every honest man; and because the custodians of these truths ordered the worship of relics, many honest people felt that they should obey. The authority which the Church had rightly used to preserve and propagate the historic Faith was wrongly used to preserve and propagate unhistorical fantasy and fiction. Christendom swallowed a lie because it was served up by the purveyors of truth.

Today the greatest authority in the world is the authority of Science. Science has put men on the moon and new hearts into old bodies. It is Science that we bless for our creation, preservation, and all the blessings of this life, but above all for the inestimable boon of television, automation, and contraception. What the Church's authority was to mediaeval Europe, that the authority of Science is to Western man. And just as Frederick the Wise accepted papal authority in matters reaching far beyond the Pope's rightful jurisdiction, so modern man has accepted the dogmas of Science regarding the origin and age of the universe, even though these are subjects quite outside the legitimate sphere of scientific investigation. The respect due to scientists for their undoubted achievements in the realm of the seen, the tangible and the predictable, has been naively transferred to their unwarranted pronouncements concerning the unseen, the intangible, and the unpredictable. The fallacy of Evolution has been swallowed because it is prescribed by many searchers after truth.

We may leave it to the historians of a later age to decide which creed requires the greatest credulity: the Gnostic belief of early centuries, the mediaeval faith in Relics, or the modern belief in "missing links" – a belief which bridges enormous gaps in the fossil record with creatures of the imagination.

What is certain is that civilization has once again been the victim of a gigantic hoax: in almost every University of the world a stupendously improbable non-fact is being taught as if it were true.

[1] II Peter 3.16,17.

CHAPTER 17

BACK TO THE BIBLE

*"Hypothetical reconstruction of major evolutionary deve-
lopments — such as that linking birds to reptiles — are
beginning to look more and more like science fiction
fantasies ...."*

M. DENTON (see Appendix A), 1985

We prefaced this book with a light-hearted poem because
the British people have been endowed with a strong vein
of humour and common sense. Isn't it time we applied
these excellent qualities to Education?

The desperate search for pedigrees of the whale, the
bat, the giraffe and a thousand other creatures, is worthy
of "Alice Through the Looking Glass". The frequent
discoveries of various shades and grades of homo sapiens
or insipiens, anthropopithecoi or pithecanthropoi, each
discovery exploding the fragile hypotheses erected upon
the last discovery, are reminiscent of Gilbertian comedy.
For entertainment and delight let us send our children to
Kipling. "How the Elephant Got His Trunk", "How the
Camel Got His Hump", "How the Rhinoceros Got His
Skin" and "How the Leopard Got His Spots", are tales
as plausible as any concocted by the solemn theorists.
But for serious history and pre-history let us turn again
to the Bible, for there alone will be found the *facts* which
explain our wonder-filled world.

Listen to Sir Winston Churchill:

"We believe that the most scientific view, the most up-
to-date and rationalistic conception, will find its fullest
satisfaction in taking the Bible story literally ... we may
be sure that all these things happened just as they are set
out in Holy Writ. We may believe that they happened to
people not so very different from ourselves, and that the

impressions those people received were faithfully recorded, and have been transmitted across the centuries with far more accuracy than many of the telegraphed accounts we read of today's events.

"Let the men of science and of learning expand their knowledge and probe with their researches every detail of the records which have been preserved to us from those dim ages. All they will do is to fortify the grand simplicity and essential accuracy of the recorded truths which have lighted so far the pilgrimage of man."[1]

[1] "Thoughts and Adventures' pp. 293–4.

APPENDIX A

In his book *Anti-Darwinian Scientists* (Philosophical Library, New York, 1987) Wendell Bird lists about fifty: here is a selection —

1) Pierre-Paul Grassé, Professor of zoology, EVOLUTION OF LIVING ORGANISMS (1977): "No matter how numerous they may be, mutations do not produce any kind of evolution."

2) G. Sermonti, Professor of genetics, University of Perugia, DOPO DARWIN: CRITICA ALL EVOLUZIONISMO (1980): "Biology will receive no advantage from following Darwin ... it must leave the blind alleys of the evolutionistic myth ..."

3) Sir Fred Hoyle & Wickramasinghe, EVOLUTION FROM SPACE (1981): "The scientific facts throw Darwin out ... but leave William Paley still in the tournament."

4) Francis Hitching, WHERE DARWIN WENT WRONG (1982): "... neo-Darwinism claims to be the unifying theory of biology, but it's nothing of the kind ..." (quoting Brian Goodwin of Sussex University).

5) Gordon R. Taylor, THE GREAT EVOLUTION MYSTERY (1983): "There are no intermediate forms between finned and limbed creatures in the fossil collections of the world."

6) Michael Pitman, ADAM & EVOLUTION (1984): "There has been neither chemical evolution nor macro-evolution. This book advocates a grand and full-blooded creation."

7) I. L. Cohen, DARWIN WAS WRONG: A STUDY IN PROBABILITIES (1984): "... if mathematics is correct, then we have to discard the present concepts of evolution."

8) EVOLUTION: A THEORY IN CRISIS (1985) by

Michael Denton, micro-biologist. (*A devastating attack on all theories of macro-evolution*). "Ultimately the Darwinian theory is no more nor less than the great cosmogenic myth of the twentieth century."

APPENDIX B

Calvin on Creation

"God was pleased that a history of the creation should exist ... the period of time is marked so as to enable the faithful to ascend by an *unbroken succession of years* (my italics) to the first origin of their race and of all things. This knowledge is of the highest use not only as an antidote to the monstrous fables which anciently prevailed in Egypt and other regions ... but also as a means of giving a clearer manifestation of the eternity of God as contrasted with the birth of creation, and thereby inspiring us with higher admiration. We must not be moved by the profane jeer that it is strange how it did not sooner occur to the Deity to create the heavens and the earth ... thousands of generations might have existed, but the present world is drawing to a close before it has completed its six thousandth year. Why God delayed so long it is neither fit nor lawful to enquire.

With the same view Moses relates that the work of creation was accomplished not in one moment, but in six days. By this statement we are drawn away from fiction to the one God who thus divided his work into six days, that we may have no reluctance to devote our whole lives to the contemplation of it."

APPENDIX C: DEMYTHOLOGIZING GENESIS

In a brilliant exposé of Bultmann's school of New Testament criticism, C. S. Lewis writes: "All theology of the liberal type involves at some point – and often involves throughout – the claim that the real behaviour and purpose and teaching of Christ came very rapidly to be misunderstood and misrepresented by His followers, and has been recovered or exhumed only by modern scholars" ('Christian Reflections'). He goes on to show that very much the same claim was made by Jowett in re-interpreting Plato, and is made "every week by a clever undergraduate, every quarter when a dull American don discovers for the first time what some Shakesperian play really meant." Lewis concludes: "The idea that any man or writer should be opaque to those who lived in the same culture, spoke the same language, shared the same habitual imagery and unconscious assumptions, and yet be transparent to those who have none of these advantages, is in my opinion preposterous. There is an *a priori* improbability in it which almost no argument and no evidence could counterbalance."

The same argument may be applied with equal force to the Old Testament, and to Genesis 1-11 in particular. Modern scholars reinterpret Moses and claim to have discovered for the first time what these chapters really mean; but it is rather more probable that the true interpretation is to be found among those who lived in the same culture, spoke the same language, shared the same habitual imagery and unconscious assumptions – in other words, the Jews. And it is certain the the Jews regarded the "days" as literal days, the Flood as universal, and the genealogies as constituting a chronology (on this point the testimony of Josephus is conclusive.)

Secondly, C. S. Lewis points out that the question – Do miracles happen? – "is a purely philosophical question. Scholars, as scholars, speak on it with no more authority than anyone else ... if one is speaking of authority, the united authority of all the biblical critics in the world counts here for nothing. On this they speak simply as men; men obviously influenced by, and perhaps insufficiently critical of, the spirit of the age they grew up in."

Similarly, on the question – Was creation an instantaneous miracle? – the united authority of all the scientists in the world counts for nothing. On this they speak simply as men; men obviously influenced by, and perhaps insufficiently critical of, the spirit of the age they grew up in.

APPENDIX D; ARE GENESIS 5 AND 11 INTENDED TO BE STRICT CHRONOLOGY?

"The Old Testament is clear in placing the date of creation somewhere within the period 5000–4000 BC. The Jewish calendar still works on this basis ...."

JAMES BARR, Regius Professor of Hebrew, Oxford University, *Escaping from Fundamentalism* (1984)

The explanation of Genesis 5 and 11 offered in the 'New Bible Dictionary' is this: that since there are gaps in the genealogy of Christ in Matthew 1, therefore we may assume that there are similar gaps in the genealogies of those chapters. This theory is open to at least three objections:

1) A fundamental principle of Scripture is its complementarity. What one book omits, another includes; what one writer narrates in full, another summarizes. The Bible is meant to be read like any other book, from the beginning to the end; and, as in any other book, that which has been clearly stated in earlier 'chapters' is assumed as known in later 'chapters'. Thus when Matthew, writing to the Jews, stated that "JORAM begat UZZIAH", he was not misleading or deceiving anyone. Probably Jewish children knew their list of kings as well as an English schoolboy knows the list of *his;* and they would immediately have spotted that three names had been omitted. They would perceive that Matthew was not attempting to give a complete genealogy, but simply to record the Messiah's pedigree in a way that is easy to remember.

On the other hand if the author of Genesis 5 and 11 has omitted names from the list, he has misled scores of generations of Jewish and Christian scholars, because there is no possible way of checking the record, and all have therefore assumed that the record is complete. Can we think that He who is the Truth would lead so many thousands, for hundreds of years, to believe a lie?

2) In any discussion of Genesis 5 and 11 the relevant NT document is not, surely, Matthew's genealogy, but Luke's (ch.3). And it seems very evident that Luke intends to give us a *complete* list of *all* the names. He gives 42 names covering the 1000 years from David to Jesus, less than 25 years per generation. Can we believe there have been any omissions here? And if there are no omissions in the first part of the genealogy, are we justified in postulating omissions in the second?

However, by far the strongest objection to the gaps-theory is this: that it makes nonsense of Scripture. For whereas all the other genealogies in the Bible consist merely of lists of names, Genesis 5 and 11 give the age of each father at the birth of his son, thus absolutely excluding the possibility of any gap. The so-called parallels in Egyptian literature are not parallel at all, for none of them mention any age before or after the father's 'begetting'. And if we deny Moses' purpose to construct a complete chronology from Adam to Joseph, we are left asking ourselves: What conceivable purpose *is* served by recording these patriarchal ages?

Positive Evidence

On the positive side the following may be urged:

1) Almost all Jewish and Christian scholars before Darwin took these chapters to be strict chronology, because they give every appearance of being such. As Prof. S. R. Driver wrote (Commentary on Genesis, 1904): "There is a systematic chronology running through the book from the beginning almost to the end, so methodically and carefully constructed that every important birth, marriage and death has its assigned place in it." Attempts are often made to drive a wedge

94

between Ussher and the Bible, as though he said one thing and the Word of God another. But this argument would be equally valid if applied to the Athanasian Creed: the doctrine of the Trinity is nowhere stated in Scripture, but it is *logically deducible* from it. Anstey (p. 67) points out that "no chronologer who has adopted the numbers in the Hebrew text has ever failed to fix the Flood 1656 years, and the death of Joseph 2369 years, after Adam's creation", because these figures, and no others, are *logically deducible* from the text. Sir Isaac Newton checked Ussher's chronology, and could find no fault with it.

2) The so-called confusion about the Septuagint and Samaritan Pentateuch is really a smoke-screen. "Most critical writers in modern times ... have decided that the numbers of the Hebrew text are the most original, and therefore the most correct, on the ground that the LXX and Samaritan texts betray systematic alterations" (JFB Commentary, p. 84). But whichever figures we accept, the indisputable fact remains that *both* Greek-speaking *and* Hebrew-speaking Jews believed this to be a chronology.

3) One very interesting fact is that, in spite of all the overlapping of the patriarchs, there was *no* overlapping at the Flood. Lamech, Noah's father, died five years before it came; and Methuselah, Noah's grandfather, died in the year of the Flood. On the strict-chronology interpretation God's timing was perfect, so that neither of the old men had to go through the ordeal. Of course this does not prove that the strict-chronology interpretation is true; but it seems to point that way.

4) Long ago Calvin perceived the purpose of these genealogies: they *are* chronology, but more than chronology. They are designed to show the continuity of revealed religion. God has had His holy prophets "since the world began" (Luke 1.70), and the continuity

95

depends on one holy prophet's life overlapping his successor's. But according to the gaps-theory Enoch could no more have talked to Methuselah than Boadicea to Queen Victoria.

Commentary on the Commentators

"No intellectual discoveries are more painful than those which expose the pedigree of ideas."

DR. L. CARMICHAEL, Secretary of the Smithsonian Institute, 1953 (quoted in TGF, p. 329).

It is instructive (though melancholy) to observe how Bible expositors have slowly but steadily been driven back from the simple and obvious interpretation of Genesis 1–11:

1) In 1824 Thomas Scott's Commentary (8th ed.) was published with a full chronology accepting Ussher's dates, Creation in six days, and the universal Flood.

2) In 1842 Dr. Gaussen of Geneva wrote: "There is no physical error in the Word of God. If there were, the book would not be from God."

3) Dr. Angus' Bible Handbook treats Genesis 5 and 11 as strict chronology (1860).

4) In 1865 Jamieson, Fausset and Brown published their Commentary, still accepting Ussher (at least in Genesis), but following Dr. Chalmers' "Gap Theory" between the first two verses of Genesis, in order to fit in the fossils *before* Adam; and following Dr. Pye Smith's "fantastic" (TGF) theory of a local flood in Mesopotamia.

5) Patrick Fairbairn's 'Imperial Dictionary of the Bible' (1885) accepts the Hebrew figures of Genesis 5 and 11 as a trustworthy chronology. The author of the article on 'Chronology' writes: "The very fact that the Septua-

gint synchronizes with the Egyptian chronology is the strongest possible testimony against the scheme followed by the Septuagint – considering the uncertain sources whence the Egyptian chronology was deduced, the principles on which it was constructed, and the disposition so strong in that people and other ancient nations of assigning a high and even fabulous date to their origin – witness the dynasties of Manetho ..."

6) By 1897 the archaeologists were quite emancipated from the Bible 'straitjacket' and were helping themselves to thousands of (imaginary) years. So we find in Ellicott's Commentary (p. 55): "Scholars have *long* acknowledged that these genealogies were never intended for chronological purposes." (our italics!)

7) Murray's Bible Dictionary (1908) gives up all pretence of claiming the authority of Christian scholars, or biblical evidence, to deny the strict-chronology interpretation. It roundly states that "*scientific* evidence demands a greater age ... civilization dates back a longer period than that allowed by Ussher before Abraham."

8) Kidner (IVF Com., 1967) accepts the life spans of the patriarchs as literal, but rejects the chronology: "Our present knowledge of civilization, e.g. at Jericho, goes back to at least 7000 B.C., and of man himself very much further" (p. 82). Mr. Kidner does not add, what is nevertheless a fact, that this "knowledge" is claimed by archaeologists who dismiss the Flood as a local inundation so small that it has left *no evidence whatever*. He goes on to suggest that "further study of the conventions of ancient genealogy may throw new light on the intention of the chapter."

Infallible but not intelligible?

This raises an important question: is there any value in professing our belief in the infallibility of Scripture if at the same time we deny its intelligibility? Does not this border on superstition? No doubt there are some obscure verses which have baffled all the commentators; but when we find 53 verses of perfectly plain statements and numbers, dare we say that these words are "infallible" if they are at the same time (to us) meaningless?

Many Hindus today will swear by the divine inspiration of their Vedas, and if you point out to them the absurdity of a world supported by an elephant standing on a tortoise they will either "spiritualize" the text or profess agnosticism on that particular point. Are we to descend to the same level of apologetic for the Bible and profess a "reverent agnosticism" about the years in Genesis 5 and 11 – hoping that some new discovery will show that the figures do not mean what all God's people before Darwin believed them to mean? Surely the more excellent way is to challenge the *human* testimony (king-lists etc.) and chemical dating methods which appear to contradict the divine testimony.

Conclusion

The "assured results" of archaeology, where they contradict the chronology of the Bible, are no more to be trusted than the "assured results" of geology. We do not maintain that belief in the date of Creation as 4004 B.C. is a necessary article of faith, but we do repudiate all the attempts of modern "science falsely so called" to reduce the figures of Genesis 5 and 11 to inexplicable doodling. Every scheme to harmonize more or less of the Bible with more or less of Science eventually produces a result more or less absurd. Uniformitarian astronomers demand billions of years for starlight to reach us; uniformitarian geologists require millions of years for rocks to form; uniformitarian biologists assume millions of years for Evolution; and uniformitarian archaeologists postulate thousands of years for languages to develop and buildings to fall down. None of them can prove their dates except on the basis of Uniformitarianism, or documents incomparably less trustworthy than the Bible. None of them can show satisfactory reasons why we should not believe what our Christian forefathers believed:

1) That the Bible is true historically, chronologically and scientifically, wherever it touches on matters of history, chronology or science.

2) That Adam and Eve, from whom we are all descended, were created on the Sixth Day, about 6000 years ago.

3) That God wiped out the 'old world' by a universal Flood, between 4000 and 5000 years ago.

"Thy word is true from the beginning."

Psalm 119, 160.

THE GREAT BRAIN
ROBBERY

PART II

".... we demolish sophistries and all that raises its proud head against the knowledge of God; we compel every human thought to surrender in obedience to Christ...."

II Corinthians 10.5 (NEB)

1   *"The Early Earth"* by DR JOHN C. WHITCOMB
(Baker Book House Co. ISBN 0 8010 9679 0 1986, $8.95,
174 pp available from reviewer at £6.00)

If you can afford only one book on Genesis, buy this one.
John Whitcomb is a scholar and a gentleman: concise,
clear, good-humoured, deeply spiritual (about 350 Scripture references), and very well-informed. Much of the
book is addressed to Christians who go along with
Darwin because they don't know enough science to
refute him, and are willing (too willing) to be persuaded
that Genesis One can be re-interpreted without destroy-
ing the fabric of Christianity. Gently, but firmly, JW
demonstrates the fallacy of this viewpoint.

Whitcomb enjoys several advantages denied to other
writers on the subject. He is co-author of one of the most
successful religious books of this century (THE GENE-
SIS FLOOD, 28 printings, many translations — the
latest into Korean) and for twenty-five years has been
fielding criticisms, corrections, misunderstanding and
ridicule. This has produced a rare maturity of outlook on
the whole question of Origins: objections are answered
with care and courtesy. Secondly, he has travelled far
and wide to mission fields, conducting seminars on
Creation at high and low theological levels all over the
world. This experience has enabled him to 'boil down'
the message to its basic elements, making it both attractive (21 excellent illustrations) and digestible to a wide
range of readers. Also, the book is right up to date.
Many, if not most, of the references are to books
published in the 1980's. In particular, JW makes good
use of two powerful critiques — ADAM AND EVOLU-
TION (1984), by Michael Pitman, and EVOLUTION: A
THEORY IN CRISIS (1985) by Michael Denton, a
professional biologist. At the same time he effectively
answers three recent salvos from the theistic-evolutionist

camp: Charles Hummel's THE GALILEO CONNEC-TION (IVP, 1986), Howard Van Till's THE FOURTH DAY (Eerdman's, 1986), and IN THE BEGINNING (IVP, 1985) by Henri Blocher. So — this is no rechauffé pot-boiler, but a vigorous contemporary defence of the Faith against 'science falsely so called'.

"Creation was supernatural — creation was sudden — creation involved a superficial appearance of age." Many analogies have been dreamed up in the attempt to bring Genesis into accord with scientific theories, but JW points out that the safest analogy is of Scripture with Scripture. Nearly all Christ's miracles were instanta-neous: water into wine, and the feeding of the 5000, are striking examples of 'appearance of age' in the finished product — but no deception. Whitcomb points out the total incompatibility of evolution with Genesis: light and botanical life before the sun; life on land before life in the sea; birds and whales before land animals; man a distinct creation, and woman made from man; all land creatures vegetarian before the Fall. He answers objections based on the 'impossible' length of the Sixth Day, and the fallacy of the 'never-ending' sabbath. He exposes the failure of evolutionary predictions and explanations in biology, geology, and palaeontology. Without elaborat-ing the detailed arguments of THE GENESIS FLOOD, he briefly shows how the Ark was large enough to carry two of all land animals, the Deluge was the cause of (nearly) all the fossils, and NT references prove it must have been worldwide. The book concludes with a scho-larly refutation of the Gap Theory.

In the Times of 3 February 1986, under the headline "BISHOPS LIKELY TO DECLARE DURHAM'S OPINIONS ON VIRGIN BIRTH LEGITIMATE", Clifford Longley wrote:

"... theologians have long assumed the licence to extract the spiritual meaning from scriptural passages, leaving behind as dross the historical detail given. To take the most obvious case, not even strict fundamentalists believe that God created the world in six intervals of 24 hours, as described in Genesis ... *By implication therefore* ((my italics)), the Church of England cannot insist on the literal acceptance of the Resurrection narratives, as if they alone were accurate ...''

JW would agree that Clifford Longley's logic is impeccable: Durham is first cousin to Darwin. Many evangelicals have lived and died in the fond delusion that evolution may be true: they will be judged by the light they had. But today, when Darwin's blindness and blunders have been exposed as never before in 130 years, it is high time for Christians to awake out of sleep and challenge the pseudo-scientific basis of all biblical criticism. The message needs to be thundered from every pulpit in England, and THE EARLY EARTH will supply enough ammunition for a year's preaching. "The God who has revealed Himself in the Lord Jesus Christ and His written Word, *cannot lie....*" (p. 161)

2 *A Chapter of Horrors*

"Dead flies cause the ointment of the perfumer to send forth a stinking savour: so doth a little folly outweigh wisdom and honour."
                                        Ecclesiastes 10.1

Just five pages out of 244 — but how they spoil the book! I refer to the chapter on Evolution in LIFE STORY: BIOLOGY FOR SCHOOL AND COLLEGE (Oliver & Boyd, 1986) by F. M. Sullivan. The rest of the 'story' seems unexceptionable, with particularly good line-drawings; but here our author loses touch with reality. To be fair, he does use cautious language: "All the vertebrates *are thought* to have evolved from simple fish-like animals ... this is *believed* to have taken over 400 million years ... some of the stages through which ... the vertebrates *may* have passed" (my italics). However, the general effect of these pages is highly misleading.

1) "Many people believe that all these species were created in their present form by God ... Scientists, however, prefer another explanation. Scientists believe ... evolution ..." Notice the subtle contrast between "people" and "scientists" — clearly implying that *all* scientists believe in evolution, and if you don't, you are not a scientist! This in spite of the fact that hundreds of scientists belong to creationist societies the world over, and some distinguished pioneers like Sir Ambrose Fleming and Sir Ernst Chaim were outspoken critics of Darwinism.

2) Almost a whole page is taken up with EVIDENCE FROM ANATOMY, the famous 'pentadactyl limb' shown in man, rabbit, bat, bird, mole and whale. This is really inexcusable. In 1971 Sir Gavin De Beer published his HOMOLOGY: AN UNSOLVED PROBLEM (OUP, A Level textbook), showing almost the same diagram but with this comment:

"It used to be assumed that similarity of structure (e.g. the bones of the forelimb) in different animals could be explained by inheritance from a common ancestor; but it is now known that such *similarity cannot be ascribed to identity* of genes" (my italics). The diagrams look very convincing, and could easily persuade youngsters; yet we know they prove *nothing* as to common ancestry.

3) "When large numbers of fossils are examined, we find what the Theory of Evolution predicts we should ..." The enormity of this 'inexactitude' can scarcely be exaggerated. Evolution predicts that there should be millions of transitional forms, as Darwin himself admitted, but in fact we find *none*. In the picture the first amphibian is separated from its "ancestor" fish by a mere three stepping stones; but all palaeontologists know that

there is in fact *no* link between finned and limbed creatures.

4) The evolution of the Horse is portrayed in five drawings which differ hardly at all except in size. A smart pupil who looks up 'HORSES' in the Guinness Book of Records will find that in Argentina within the last thirty years they have been bred down to 26 lbs and up to nearly 3000 lbs — all the same species, EQUUS! As Professor Heribert-Nilsson has written: "... the family tree of the horse is beautiful and continuous only in the textbooks."

5) "For many years no connection could be found between the birds and the reptiles from which they are thought to have evolved. Eventually, however, fossils of animals which seemed to represent a halfway stage between the two were discovered."

This is the exact opposite of the truth. In fact Archaeopteryx was discovered in 1862, only three years after Darwin's 'Origin', and was hailed with glee as *the* reptile-bird link — until 1977 when a 'real' bird was found at the same level in Utah, followed by the discovery of another real bird "75 million years older" by Dr Sankar Chatterjee of Texas Tech. on 13 August, 1986. So what was *thought* to be the connection has been proved to be no connection at all. As Dr Raup of the Chicago Field Museum wrote in 1979: "We have *even* fewer examples of evolutionary transition than we had in Darwin's time ..."

6) To crown it all, we have "NATURAL SELECTION IN THE PEPPERED MOTH" — the usual pictures with the usual comment, all very true but quite irrelevant. What is *not* pointed out is the obvious fact that this is merely micro-evolution or (better) variation within the species, no more significant than the difference between Negroid and white races. A moth is a moth is a moth. Yet, as so often, the change from a light to a dark

majority population is alleged to be evidence for the truth of macro-evolution!

***

To sum up: this chapter demonstrates the total bankruptcy of Darwin's Theory in the 1980's. If there were better arguments at hand, Sullivan must surely have used them. As it is, using the powerfully suggestive force of pictures, he has not scrupled to mislead youthful readers by hypotheses long since exploded and out of date. The only real weight behind evolution is the weight of *authority*, so this card is carefully played first (see para. 1 above) to silence opposition.

3 *The Blind Watchmaker* by RICHARD DAWKINS, 1986, Longmans Group UK Ltd. 332 pages. £12.95 Longman House, Burnt Mill, Harlow, Essex CM20 2JE

Reading this book reminds me of a little rhyme made up by the students of Balliol College in the 1870's:

> First come I: my name is Jowett,
> There's no knowledge but I know it.
> I am the Master of this College:
> What I don't know isn't knowledge.

A certain air of omniscience still emanates from Oxford dons: one gets the impression that even if the author himself does not quite know everything, yet Dawkins + friends + colleagues together come very close to encyclopaedic learning. To be compared with Galileo (back cover blurb) is enough to turn the head of any scientist; so the reader must brace himself to resist intimidation.

Dawkins (hereafter RD) is a full-blooded Darwinian evolutionist, a missionary with a gospel to proclaim to benighted Lamarckians, creationists, theists, nay, even to deists. He is Richard the Lion-Heart, attacking the armies of 'infidels' who espouse the Argument from Personal Incredulity and refuse to believe (e.g.) that spiders' webs could have evolved by minute modifications over millions of years. His reply to this heresy is simple:

"I, Richard Dawkins, have some experience of spiders and their webs ... and I firmly believe that the web could have been produced step by step through random variation" (in other words, the Argument from Personal Credulity). So, what RD believes must be true, with or without evidence. Living as he does in the post-Christian era, he can afford to be much bolder than Darwin, — who had to tread cautiously through the Victorian religious minefield. He admits he writes as an advocate as well as a scientist — which reminds me of the story of a famous Greek advocate who allowed a friend to read over the speech he was going to make on behalf of a client. "The first time I read it," said the friend, "I thought it excellent. The second time I thought less of it, and the third time it seemed full of flaws." "Ah, maybe, but the judge will hear it only once!" replied Demosthenes. Dawkins' WATCHMAKER is more a brief than a textbook, and the oftener one reads it the more tricks of advocacy are discovered — special pleading, begging the question, false analogies, demolition of straw men, imputing guilt by association (with Jehovah's Witnesses), denigration of opponents, and withholding of vital evidence. He is most persuasive when playing with computers, and least convincing when writing about real live animals.

It was Dr Samuel Johnson, I think, who remarked that "one may scold a carpenter who has made you a bad table, though you cannot make a table. It is not your trade to make tables." Nor is biology my trade, but I don't have to be a biologist to notice facts ignored or misconstrued. When RD says that "no serious biologist

109

doubts the fact that evolution has happened, nor that all living creatures are cousins of one another", one has to assume that he reads only those authors who agree with him. Michael Denton's EVOLUTION: A THEORY IN CRISIS completely refutes that allegation, and one might have expected RD to make some attempt at answering Denton's objections; but the book is not so much as mentioned. Not a single modern creationist book is listed in the bibliography; even G. R. Taylor's THE GREAT EVOLUTION MYSTERY is excluded. RD gives no references for his quotations ... perhaps just a matter of style, but unfortunate when the quote happens to be inaccurate. The opening paragraph of the book states:

"... our own existence is a mystery no longer because ... Darwin *and Wallace* solved it ..." (emphasis added)

In fact, of course, Wallace did *not* agree with Darwin about the Descent of Man from Monkey; he believed natural selection could not account for man himself, thus provoking Darwin to protest:

"I differ grievously from you and I am very sorry for it. I hope you have not murdered too completely your own and my child."

Dawkins' inexactitude, at the threshold of a scientific treatise, does not inspire confidence.

Now we shall look at some of the methods by which RD seeks to persuade the world that Darwin got it right, utterly, gloriously right, whereas poor old William Paley was "wrong, utterly, gloriously wrong"! Fortune favours the bold, so he begins by directing our attention to one of the most complex systems in all Nature — echolocation in bats. By describing this in some detail he elicits our awe and wonder; but then, *instead of explaining* how it could/must have evolved by infinitesimally small stages, he wades in to attack the Bishop of Birmingham's THE PROBABILITY OF GOD. This book includes (a) an

110

exceedingly weak argument against the whiteness of polar bears being due to natural selection: RD has no difficulty in refuting it. (b) a paragraph on spiders' webs (see above) (c) a paragraph on eyes, which RD answers thus: "Eyes don't fossilize ..." It is hard to believe he did not know this statement is untrue. One of the most impressive pages of THE GREAT EVOLUTION MYSTERY describes the discovery of fossilized trilobite eyes by Levi-Setti and Clarkson in 1973. Right at the bottom of the ladder of life, among the most 'primitive' of all creatures, we find absolute perfection of material (calcite, chitin) and of mathematical construction. Why was this very important piece of evidence omitted from RD's assessment? He goes on to brood over the difficulty we have in imagining geological time. "In a few thousand years we have gone from wolf to Pekinese ... think of the total quantity of change involved in going from wolf to Chihuahua, and then multiply it by the number of walking paces between London and Baghdad. This will give some idea of the amount of change that we can expect in real natural evolution." Here is a classic example of false analogy, for the following reasons:

1) there is no evidence that dogs were originally bred from wolves. Historical records in every ancient civilization mention them as distinct species from the beginning.

2) all freaks such as Chihuahuas are *man*-made, artificial breeds. They would never survive in the wild; so there is no true parallel with "natural evolution".

3) are we to believe that because we now, after 2000 years of breeding, have dogs as diverse as the Great Dane and the Peke, therefore by 4000 AD we shall have dogs weighing a ton, and others weighing *one ounce*? Extrapolation is a risky sport: all farmers know there is a limit to breeding, both up and down. So it is highly misleading to use this analogy to 'prove' that anything can be changed into anything, given enough time.

Another argument in the Bishop's book is the Cuckoo Story. Canon C. E. Raven, a fine ornithologist of the 1930's, pointed out that cuckoos require (a) a mother who won't build her own nest but lays her egg in others' (b) a chick that will turf out other chicks and eggs from its host-parents' nest, (c) a foster-mother willing to feed the monstrous murderer of her own chicks. For the system to work, says Raven, "the whole 'opus perfectum' must have been achieved simultaneously." Not so! replies RD. "It isn't true that each part is essential for the success of the whole." But instead of showing *how* the system could have developed bit by bit, *he walks right away* from the whole question, and contents himself with the feeble unsupported assertion that "... a simple, rudimentary ... cuckoo parasitism system, is better than none at all." Since it is obvious that a chick that pushes his *own* brothers and sisters out of the nest would be *worse* than none at all, even a non-ornithologist might be tempted to doubt whether Professor Dawkins has thought this one through. It is Canon Raven, we opine, who is utterly, gloriously right.

Meanwhile all this peripheral argumentation has diverted our attention from the central problem of bat-evolution: how did a ground-mammal ever become an air-mammal? RD entirely omits two vital facts:
1) the oldest bat-fossil skeleton is exactly the same as a modern bat's, bone for bone; (2) all bats have their pelvis twisted 180° from that of ground mammals, and no fossil ever discovered shows any sign of a 90° or any other degree of twist. What has happened to all the intermediates? The question is not even raised. So, in the chapter GOOD DESIGN, after 20 pages expounding the marvels of echolocation, the 'proof' that this evolved from nothing is reduced to the meagre proposition that half a loaf is better than no bread, half an ear better than no

ear, *therefore* echolocation and the bat must have been evolved, not created!

What about the famous bombardier beetle? Here is RD's explanation: "The bombardier beetle's ancestors simply pressed into service chemicals that already happened to be around. That's often how evolution works." Translated into human terms this could be: "My 6-year old *simply* pressed into service some loose gunpowder and metal that *happened* to be around, constructed a double-barrelled 12-bore gun and cartridges, and fired them at the burglar." (children are much more intelligent than beetles). A tall story; but no taller, we think, than RD's fantasy. And why is the world not overrun with bombardier beetles, if its armament is so easy to make, so effective in use?

It is refreshing to find *one* phenomenon of zoology that remains a mystery even to our learned Professor. This is the periodical cicada which divides into three species, and each species has both a 17-year and a 13-year variety. All attempts to explain this in terms of evolution have failed. Why not 10, 11, 12, 14, 15, 16, 18, or *any* number of years? and why have not all three species been ousted by the much faster-breeding two-year and five-year species (not mentioned by RD)? By the Darwinian law of differential reproduction, the race is to the swift and the battle to the baby-boomers. But here the slow are equally successful, and show no signs of becoming extinct. Once again the mysterious balance of nature points to an all-wise Creator whose arbitrary arrangements defy human analysis.

RD takes a whole chapter to explain what he calls the 'arms race' between cheetah and gazelle, each animal running faster and faster (another Just So story) to catch or escape being caught. How much more convincing the theory would be if fossils had ever been found of a slow cheetah or a slow gazelle. But RD is very economical

113

indeed in his references to fossils ... and he leaves untouched the far more basic problem: why should any animal *become* carnivorous when surrounded by an abundance of vegetable food which requires *no* catching?

Throughout the book, superficial resemblances are stressed and real difficulties are evaded. When trying to persuade us that fish turned into amphibians, RD talks about different kinds of lung but says not a word about the revolution in *skeletal* design that was necessary to enable a fish to walk on four feet — a revolution for which, of course, there is not one scrap of evidence, living or dead. Likewise the transformation of an amphibian egg into an amniotic (reptilian) egg — involving eight separate 'improvements' — is nowhere discussed. Again, he asks, How did wings get their start? — then goes on to wing *flaps*, as if they could automatically be turned into proper wings with feathers! The origin of feathers is not even mentioned. Snake venom gets the same treatment. "There is a continuous graded series from ordinary spit to deadly venom." So ... 'once upon a time the cobra was a beautiful harmless creature ...' — or was it? RD makes no attempt to explain what *advantage* accrued to the poisonous snake by reason of its poison, when it is obvious to all the world that non-poisonous ones have survived and multiplied just as well as their dangerous 'cousins'. In fact 92% of all snakes are non-poisonous. The Blind Watchmaker that produced the other 8% must have been not only blind but barmy. (The creationist, of course, has quite different and satisfactory reasons for the existence of venom in some snakes).

Much space is devoted to 'convergence', a word invented to disguise the fact that evolution cannot account for similarities in unrelated creatures. Flight technology and sonar are supposed to have been 'discovered' quite independently by several kinds of animal. But if these extraordinary powers were acquired independently, why should not the corti and every other piece of specialist equipment have been invented ten, twenty or 100 times? Wriggle as he may, RD cannot prevent us from seeing that sonar is explicable only as God's gift to bird, bat and dolphin for their particular needs in different environments. And if the common possession of extra-ordinary faculties does not point to a 'common ancestry', why should the possession of 'ordinary' faculties prove it? Why should not the Creator have given to all vertebrates *independently* that very useful organ, a backbone? When he comes to DNA, RD says that human genes' 99% similarity to chimpanzees' must prove our close cousinship and common ancestry. He overlooks the fact that (a) this may well be another case of 'convergence', and (b) there is a wide variation of DNA among frogs, which "proves" that we are nearer to chimps than frogs are to frogs!

RD boldly repeats Darwin's challenge:

"If it could be demonstrated that any complex organ existed which could not possibly have been formed by numerous successive slight modifications, my theory would absolutely break down ..."

but overlooks the fact that instincts, though invisible, are just as really part of an animal as an organ, and need explanation no less. Hence, he leaves bird-migration severely alone. It is easy to say that a short flight would be better than none, and a bird *might* be naturally selected by being able to fly one mile further than his fellow-bird. It is absolutely impossible to say that an experimental flight of ten miles from Alaska towards Hawaii would be better than none, for an American golden plover. The bird would certainly drown — *unless* it had the capacity to cover the 3000 miles non-stop, with correct navigation, the *very first time it tried*. When the penalty of failure is death, all theories of trial and error can be immediately discarded.

115

Coming to sexual selection, RD fills twenty pages of solid print to "prove" the reasonableness of the black widow bird having evolved an 18-inch tail. This is a lot easier, of course, than explaining the peacock or the Argus pheasant, whose tails are much more conspicuous and an encumbrance to flight. Even so, it cannot be said that RD has succeeded, because the anomalies of the bird-world are legion and (it seems) wholly arbitrary. Tailless birds find mates just as easily as black widows; crows reproduce no less plentifully than peacocks; birds that nest in tree-tops have no more progeny than ground-nesters. There seems to be absolutely no correlation between beauty, brains and babies. Why are ducks and drakes different, but male and female swans indistinguishable? To these and a thousand other questions there is no answer except, "God made them like that!" RD's abstract reasoning avails nothing against (e.g.) the field-evidence adduced by Norman Macbeth (*Darwin Re-tried*, 1971), who concludes:

"Have the birds, through their patterns of sexual choice, established a system in which the race is not to the swift and the battle is not to the strong? If so, they have shaken the whole structure of Darwinism."

The next chapter is PUNCTURING PUNCTUA-TIONISM and it will be interesting to hear Stephen J. Gould's reaction to RD's thesis — that there is no real difference between the two schools of thought: in fact, punctuationists are gradualists in disguise! This is a familiar ploy in politics. If your party feels threatened, form a coalition against the Enemy. In this case the enemy are creationists, and at all costs they must not be allowed to overthrow the Establishment. To an impartial observer it seems obvious that the gradualists are right in pointing out that Nature knows nothing of 'hopeful monsters', and the punctuationists are right in retorting that the fossil record knows nothing of gradual evolution. Each group can clearly see the beam in the other's eye, and each group is blind to its own.

The climax of RD's fallacious thinking is reached in these words: "The genetic code is universal. I regard this as near-conclusive proof that all organisms are descended from a common ancestor." So — what kind of world would he *expect* to find if a Creator had populated it with a variety of creatures who all need to breathe the same air, enjoy the same sunlight, drink the same water and eat (somewhat) similar kinds of food? Must a horse have six legs to prove it is no relation of the cow? (In fact, of course, evolutionists cannot even account for the different digestive systems of these animals). Ought we to expect apples to use one kind of photosynthesis, and oranges another? But, to quote Michael Denton, "... the new molecular approach to biological relationships could potentially have provided very strong, if not irrefutable, evidence supporting evolutionary claims ... all that was necessary to demonstrate an evolutionary relationship was to examine the proteins and show that the sequences could be arranged into an evolutionary series." In fact, "... the molecules reaffirm the traditional view that the system of nature conforms fundamentally to a highly ordered hierarchic scheme from which all direct evidence for evolution is *emphatically absent*." (emphasis added) So, what RD regards as the strongest evidence *for* evolution is considered by a specialist in this field to be decisive evidence *against* it.

RD's crowning unwisdom is to out-Darwin Darwin in atheism. Whereas Charles postulated "... life breathed into a few forms ... or one" by the Creator, RD will not allow the Creator even one finger in the pie. To set the ball rolling 'in the beginning' required no one and nothing, only the laws of physics. One is reminded of Francis Bacon: "... a little philosphy inclineth man's mind to atheism; but depth in philosphy bringeth men's

117

minds about to religion." The whole book illustrates the fact that Darwinism is a folk-religion, an object of genuine piety (loyalty to the Guru), and passionate devotion, on the part of its disciples. RD is unable to show any hard evidence for the evolution of the eye, the ear, echolocation, long tails, or indeed of life itself; but unshakeable faith in the great god Natural Selection lends wings to his imagination and carries him soaring into Cloud-Cuckoo-Land. Notionally he peoples the world with intermediates between humans and chimps, and seriously suggests that we have been spared many headaches by not having to discriminate (in law) between various levels of ape-men. "It is just sheer luck that these embarrassing intermediates happen not to have survived." No evidence is offered that any of them even existed: it is simply *assumed* that Lucy & Co. were a thriving company. Unsurprisingly no mention is made of Piltdown Man, Nebraska Man, Java Man, and all the other failures.

One great virtue of this book is to demonstrate the incompatibility of Darwinism and theism. RD points out the inconsistency of those sophisticated theologians who wish to appear in step with modern science, while at the same time retaining a corner for God in their cosmogony. But the great weakness of THE BLIND WATCH-MAKER is its total failure to come to grips with creationism and deal seriously with the objections to evolution. "It would obviously be *unfairly* easy to demolish some particular version of this theory ((that life was created)) ..." — thus he excuses himself from entering the tournament, because, forsooth, no foe is worthy of his steel! Instead, he uses ridicule: "... the Genesis story has no more special status than the belief of a West African tribe that the world was created from the excrement of ants." So — from Olympian heights our professional zoologist dismisses in a sentence those magnificent chapters which men of real genius like Bacon, Newton, Boyle, *and* Galileo, were content to receive as divine revelation, which Christ himself quoted as literally and historically true, and which the finest scholars of Europe, masters of ancient lore, have recognized as superior beyond comparison to all rival cosmogonies. In a last desperate attempt to win support for his party, RD besmirches the motives of his opponents. They are all either cranks (Bible-thumpers), snobs (who don't relish kinship with monkeys), or journalists (making a quick buck by attacking the Establishment). The idea that some anti-evolutionists may actually be interested in *truth*, never seems to have crossed his mind. So writers like Macbeth, Denton, and Geoffrey Harper, who are neither Bible-thumpers nor snobs nor journalists, — yet disbelievers in Darwinism — are kept carefully locked in the cupboard.

RD is an elegant writer — humorous, satirical, sparkling with felicitous comparisons. It is just an enormous pity that these golden gifts should be wasted in defence of the indefensible, in keeping the life-support system going on a body of pseudo-scientific ideas which must soon join Ptolemaic astronomy and phlogiston in the Mausoleum for Extinct Hypotheses. As Fred Hoyle has written, William Paley is still in the tournament, with a chance, a very *good* chance, of being the ultimate winner.

4 *Cross-Currents: Interactions Between Science and Faith* by COLIN A. RUSSELL (IVP, 1985, 272 pp.)

Colin Russell is Professor of the History of Science at the Open University, which is firmly committed to the dogma of Evolution. He is also a Christian, as are the publishers; so we watch with interest to see how a theistic evolutionist handles this important subject. Earlier this year we welcomed IVP's CREATION AND EVOLU-

TION, which allowed three distinguished creationists to state their position — most effectively; but Russell (CR from now on), alas, seems to have taken a step backwards from toleration and balance. As one reviewer put it, he has "no time" for creationists, in more senses than one. Of course in a book covering 24 centuries we cannot expect full coverage of a movement which has sprung into full vigour only in the past 24 years; but we might have expected something better than to see the whole debate swept under the carpet. For this summary dismissal CR alleges four reasons:

1. "... it is a peculiarly American phenomenon."
2. "... it has been extensively criticized in several recent books."
3. "... mainly because it is best illuminated indirectly by ... the earlier episodes associated with Darwin."
4. "... the current situation is confused by association with right-wing North American politics."

Let us take a closer look at these:

1. The statement is obviously untrue. CR seems strangely unaware that there was an Evolution Protest Movement in Britain 30 years before Henry Morris appeared on the scene, and there are now strong independent organisations in Australia, Korea, India, Japan, Germany, Holland, Spain, South Africa, plus two British groups headed by university Professors. Creationist literature is published in 18 major languages, including Russian. Granted, the first big 'push' came from the USA; but those who pooh-poohed D. L. Moody in the 1860's, and Billy Graham in the 1940's, had to admit later that they had failed to read the signs of the times. "Can any good thing come out of America?" Yes!

2. Among recent books "extensively criticizing" creationism, Philip Kitcher's ABUSING SCIENCE is one of the best known — published (not surprisingly) by the Open University. CR assumes that the criticisms are

well-founded, but many competent scientists think otherwise. Robert Clinkert, a Superintendent of Schools, whose doctoral thesis was in the Philosophy of Science, concludes his 23 page review with these words:

"Kitcher's book reveals that the anti-creationist movement is resorting to deception and sophistry as debate strategies."

Almost every Christian pioneer movement has been criticized in its early stages, from Peter's association with Cornelius to the China Inland Mission and William Booth. 68 years ago a newly-formed breakaway student group was extensively criticized by those who chose to remain within the Student Christian Movement. The new group was ignored and ridiculed, but God was with them, and today they are the UCCF/IVP. Let those who in their turn are tempted to criticize and ridicule, ponder the lessons of church history.

3. The idea that modern creationism is *best* illuminated from Victorian times is a subjective notion that has to be proved, not taken for granted. The Irish Question cannot be solved by Mr Gladstone's speeches in the 1880's, nor the Evolution Question by early converts to Darwinism. Time marches on, and nowhere so fast as in science. But CR has drunk deep at James R. Moore's POST-DARWINIAN CONTROVERSIES 1870–1900 and seeks to wrest from' this ancient battle-field proof that one can *now*, in 1985, be at the same time both a good Calvinist *and* a good Darwinian. (It is a pity that CR has not read, or shows no acquaintance with, Prof. John Whitcomb's trenchant review of Moore in Grace Theological Journal, Spring 1981. Whitcomb shows that Moore blunders hopelessly as an amateur theologian).

CR introduces Henry Drummond (2 pages) and Charles Kingsley (3pp) as earnest Christians who accepted evolution; and (trump card) no less than four pages are devoted to proving that Charles H. Spurgeon failed "to launch a sustained onslaught on evolution". Therefore, we are left to conclude, modern evangelicals have no right to rush in where the Metropolitan Tabernacle 'angel' feared to tread.

The fallacy of all this reasoning lies, of course in the 100 years' interval and the total failure of Darwin's predictions to be substantiated by transitional fossils, breeding experiments, and especially by microbiology (M. Denton's EVOLUTION: A THEORY IN CRISIS administers the coup de grace). If Spurgeon had read THE GENESIS FLOOD and other creationist books, I have no doubt that he too (like the present incumbent of the Met. Tab.) would have perceived that evolution is indeed 'the great brain robbery'. When millions of children are being force-fed with lies in the name of Science, would he have stayed silent?

All this Victoriana acts as a smokescreen to keep out of sight scientists like Prof. W. R. Thompson F.R.S., who had the courage (1956) to denounce Darwinism as unhelpful to biological research; Douglas Dewar, whose TRANSFORMIST ILLUSION (1957) has never been refuted; and many others. In the Epilogue, Michael Faraday is portrayed as a model Christian scientist, but even here CR grinds his axe to hew creationists. Faraday was "reticent about reconciling science and Scripture ... there is little evidence that he was in the least troubled by earlier speculation about the age of the earth, the universality of the flood, or even pre-Darwinian ideas on evolution." So, if this great man never attacked Darwin, how dare we lesser mortals do so? — that is clearly CR's message.

Contrariwise, looking back on Church History we find that the Holy Spirit seems to emphasize different truths at different times, and even the best leaders have blind spots. So it is possible that Faraday's attitude to science/ Scripture may have been less than perfect; but in any case, to his own Master he stands or falls. *We* shall be judged by a different standard, enjoying as we do the benefit of hindsight and the researches of many who have exposed the frauds and fallacies of Darwinism.

4. "... confused by right-wing politics." Another case of misinformation. Over the past five years I have attended many creation conferences, seminars and lectures in the USA, and I have never heard a word about politics. Granted, it is a standard trick of American anti-creationists to make capital out of Ronald Reagan's anti-evolutionary pronouncements, and Jerry Falwell's. But to reject creationism because these gentlemen favour it would be about as sensible as to reject Newton's Principia because he was a Tory.

Now let us turn to some other features which invite comment:

5. The great name of Calvin is invoked on the side of a non-literal interpretation of Genesis, but it is certain from his Commentary that he was a literalist of the literalists. One quotation will suffice:

"... audacious scribblers have no axiom more plausible than that faith must be free and unfettered, so that it may be possible, by reducing everything to a matter of doubt, to render Scripture flexible (so to speak) as a nose of wax." (p. xxviii) Also, it is entirely gratuitous to assume that Robert Boyle (p. 150) would have been persuaded (that I say not deceived) by the specious argumentation of Darwinian geologists and biologists. Boyle's science was experimental, practical and useful — totally different in kind from their unverifiable hypotheses and extrapolation.

6. Perhaps the most surprising omission in a book by a science *historian* is his treatment of Henry Morris, who suddenly appears — like Melchizedek, without genealogy or antecedents — in 1974 as the author of THE TROUBLED WATERS OF EVOLUTION. Morris's much better known and more influential THE GENESIS

FLOOD, co-authored with Prof. John Whitcomb in 1961 and reprinted 28 times, is not even mentioned. No attempt is made to answer its massive, cumulative arguments for a universal Flood. For CR the last word on this subject was spoken by Adam Sedgwick 150 years ago in his "recantation".

Darwin's biography, which every schoolboy knows, is rehearsed yet again (4 pages), whereas Morris is dismissed in 8 lines. The formation of the Creation Research Society, the university debates of the 1970's, the world-wide proliferation of creationism — all these are passed over in silence, a silence all the more inexplicable when one finds that CR is right up to date on the Bishop of Durham and Don Cupitt.

7. Worse still, the last chapter's title is FLOODTIDE. Here CR quotes Madame Pompadour's absurd remark, 'After me the deluge', and repeats this *mis*application of Scripture with regard to the "deluge" of scientific information by which "all familiar features are swept away and civilization is submerged and all but destroyed just as in the days of Noah." Thus the real, sudden, destruction of a wicked world — adduced by the Lord Jesus Christ as a *true* parallel to His coming again — is likened by a *false* parallel to the slow changes wrought over many decades by discoveries and inventions ... an analogy wholly misconceived and misleading. CR also calls a nuclear holocaust "the ultimate tragedy for the human race", forgetting, perhaps, that it is exactly what the Apostle Peter foretold for the End of the World — not with a whimper but a bang. The reader is lulled into a false sense of security and might well address the author as follows:

"OK — some Christians were good scientists; but obviously the first chapters of the Bible are not (according to you) literally true. So why should the last chapters be? You interpret the beginning of the Book non-literally and I interpret the end non-literally. What's the difference? Heaven and Hell — you make your own, here on earth, that's all there is. All that stuff about gates of gold and lakes of fire is picturesque symbolism for primitive people who couldn't tell the difference between fact and fiction ... just like your six-day creation, Adam's rib, Noah's flood — the lot. You have accepted science's picture of the past as correct: I accept science's picture of the future. That's logical, isn't it?''

5 *Biblical Creation and the Theory of Evolution* by DOUGLAS SPANNER, Paternoster Press, Exeter 1987, 191pp. £6.95.

Welcome to another broadside from that famous school of theistic evolution, the Research Scientists' Christian Fellowship! We are reminded of similar books by Mackay, Berry, Russell and (collaterally) Kidner and Blocher. Sir Alan Boyd (in the blurb) unwittingly exposes their weakness when he writes: 'This book is for those who look for an *expert* to guide them' (my emphasis). The assumed equation seems to be: good scientist = good theologian. In fact the opposite may be true, because of the fundamental difference between Science and Theology. In science, what is newest is often truest; in Christianity 'there can be no important truth which is not ancient ...' (Pearson, 1680). We applaud Dr. Spanner's aim to remove stumbling blocks for his unbelieving colleagues, but sincerity is not enough. His usual method is to circumvent unambiguous texts (e.g. Gen. 1:29, vegetarianism, Acts 17:26, unity of the race) and reach the opposite conclusion by devious by-paths, secondary inferences, and far-fetched analogies. Darwin's phrase, 'I can see no difficulty...' finds many an echo here. He denies:

creation in six days;
the sabbath as a memorial;
special creation of Adam, the first man;
special creation of Eve, the first woman;
Adam and Eve the progenitors
of the whole race;
perfection of the primal
creation;
changes in Nature after the Fall;
pains of childbirth as a
punishment for sin;
human death a result of the fall;
universal Flood a punishment
for universal wickedness.

Let us glance at a few of these:

1. He asserts that the primal creation was 'very good' only *relatively* because Canaan is described as a 'good' land when it was "occupied by fierce aliens' (p. 52). The answer is easy: the same verse that calls Canaan 'good' also lists six hostile tribes, so it is clear that the 'goodness' refers *only* to the fertility of the land, not to the character of its inhabitants. But in Gen. 1:31 there are *no* qualifications whatever, although – according to the author – the 'goodness' included cancer and leprosy, rabies and tetanus, syphilis and A.I.D.S. *plus* floods and fires, earthquakes and eruptions, tornados and lightning, poisonous snakes and man-eating tigers. A perfect world indeed! He drags in Romans 11:33 to cover these horrors with a blanket of inscrutability, but fails to see that it is not God's wisdom that is in question but His *righteousness*. The whole Bible cries aloud that man's sin, not God's whim, is the cause of disease and disaster; but I have found not a single reference to the *wrath* of God.

2. He 'explains' the creation of Eve as a dream. The alleged analogy is God's appearance to Solomon (1

Kings 3); but we may note that the verb in the Septuagint is 'ophthe' – the same as that used in 1 Cor. 15 for the Resurrection appearances. Does this prove that Christ's appearances were only 'spiritual', not physical? The obvious fact is that Genesis records seven famous dreams and *calls* them dreams. What conceivable motive would Moses have for *not* calling Adam's experience a dream, if it was? The crowning anomaly is his quoting of Matthew Henry, who believed completely in the literal miracle (as did Christ – Mark 10): '... the woman was dust double-refined ...' But according to the dream-theory Adam and Eve were both born naturally, with *no* refinement!

This brings us to another novelty. 'It was natural (and intended)', he writes 'that popular Israel should understand the "days" as ... of 24 hours ... But when God had given mankind further insights into the nature of the physical world, it became permissible, and indeed right, to think in more sophisticated terms.' Wait a minute! If God deliberately deceived Israel in 1400 B.C. by giving them a false, miracle-packed cosmogony suited to their 'primitive' understanding, how do we know that the record of New Testament miracles is not equally false, geared to first century superstitions but quite outmoded in the Space Age? (see *THE MYTH OF GOD INCAR-NATE*, passim).

3. He labours to prove that the Flood was only local. He ignores Gen. 9:15 (as does Kidner) and Isaiah 54:9, which refute his thesis. (Within recorded history *local* floods have drowned myriads of people: does God break His promises?) No attempt is made to expound 2 Peter 3:5,6, another passage decisive for a global deluge. Nor does he answer the 'six basic arguments' of *THE GENE-SIS FLOOD* (1961). The subject is important because St. Peter predicts that denial of the *Flood* will character-ise 'scoffers' in the last days.

(An ominous foot note is to be found in the new *TIMES ATLAS OF THE BIBLE*, 1987; Mt. Ararat *does not appear* on any map! Post-Christian academics have expunged the very word that reminds them of judgment).

What a pity that such an earnest and erudite Christian should thus 'torture texts to make them confess the creed of science', when that very creed is being demolished by many scientists who are *not* Christians!

6 *Creation or Evolution – A False Antithesis?* by M. W. POOLE & G. J. WENHAM 1987, Latimer Studies 23/24 84 pp £3.00 ISBN 0 946307 22 9/23 7

Michael Poole (MP) is a science lecturer at King's College, London, and Dr Gordon Wenham (GW) is the author of a new commentary on Genesis. They have teamed up to produce yet another defence of theistic evolution (TE), following those of Professors Mackay, Berry, Spanner, Russell, Burke, Fraser, and other members of the Research Scientists Christian Fellowhsip (RSCF). But why so many — often quoting each other and repeating the same arguments? The answer seems to be found at the end of this book: they are deeply *disturbed* by the success of creationism world-wide. Specially singled out for disapproval is Sylvia Baker's BONE OF CONTENTION ... 170,000 copies sold in five languages, and a Chinese version going into print. Clearly the movement is getting out of hand, and threatens to sweep multitudes of guileless Christians into its net!

Science

An odd feature is the absence of any discussion of biological evolution, and no mention is made of the large number of anti-evolution books written by non-Christians in recent years (see Appendix A). To ignore these, or lightly dismiss them with, "problems and difficulties are not confined to biology. They are characteristic of all the sciences ..." is a little naive, especially since MP later compares evolution with the law of gravity. (How many books have been written refuting Newton's discovery?)

MP's strategy is to leave Darwin severely alone, knowing him to be vulnerable, and concentrate attack on creationist arguments for a Young Earth. He quotes generously from the Journal of the ASA (American equivalent of the RSCF) but seems unaware of the existence of the Creation Research Society Quarterly, which for 25 years has been as important for the evolution debate as the BMJ is for medicine. Thus he makes much ado about the 'fallacy of the shrinking sun', but ignores a defence of the theory in the CRSQ March 1987. He knows nothing of the 'Age of the Earth' Conference, Pittsburgh 1986; and fails to perceive that even if the earth *were* 5 billion years old, that would not prove the truth of Darwinism, which is what the book is supposed to be about.

Mr Valiant For Truth (VFT)

By way of introducing GW's non-literal interpretation of Gen.1–3, MP indulges in a skit which can only be described as unfortunate. Mr VFT is protrayed as a zealous 'lunatic' who in the 17th C. insists that Galileo is wrong because the Bible teaches that the moon is self-luminous. This is bad science, bad scholarship, and bad use of Scripture. John Bunyan named his famous character from the AV rendering of Jeremiah 9.3. In the allegory VFT is the author of 'He who would valiant be ...' and the hero of that passage which concludes '... all the trumpets souded for him on the other side', one of the finest in English literature. *This* is the man (fictional, yes, but representing a host of real saints, including Hugh Latimer himself) whom MP chooses to ridicule! And what of the science? It is equally defective, because the opacity of the moon, and its eclipsing of the sun, were known to Greek astronomers 2000 years before Galileo. Poole's VFT is a man of straw, and the scenario a figment of his imagination. It may not be inapposite to recall that VFT's assailants were Wild-Head, Inconsiderate, and Pragmatic (= meddlesome, in Bunyan's day)!

Wenham on Genesis 1–3

GW relates these 80 verses to Near Eastern culture and tries to persuade himself, though not without hesitation, that they are compatible with evolution. For example he insists that "the world started perfect from God's hand", but does not explain what he means by 'perfect'. Does it include diseases, disasters, and death? It sounds as though he would like to answer No; but here MP takes over and affirms that "we are not told how different the world was before the Fall. The Bible says that the world was made with the possibility of going wrong (Romans 8.20) ..." (a peculiar paraphrase, which will not commend itself to Greek scholars).

In general GW follows Henri Blocher (IN THE BEGINNING, IVP), and the Literary Framework Theory, which was refuted in the 1800's by Keil & Delitzsch. At the same time he clings to Hugh Miller's (1860) idea that the Record of the Rocks actually agrees with Genesis ("not unlike"), in spite of the glaring discrepancies which have been pointed out numberless times by creationists *and* evolutionists. On the genealogies he has some novel theories, but fails to note that the whole OT has a chronology right down to the Captivity. His strangest suggestion, perhaps, is that the "chronology" of the Six Day Creation "is more of a didactic device than directly historical" because "the Hebrews were as well aware as we are" that light comes from the sun. In other words, since the account runs contrary to experience, therefore the whole narrative is non-historical! But of course all miracles run contrary to experience. By parity of reasoning one might argue that since the Jews were well aware that water is not wine, there never was a Wedding at Cana (which is just what modernist interpreters of John 2 *do* say).

It is interesting to observe our authors' bias when it comes to citing authorities. On creationism, MP quotes the scornful criticisms of Prof. Gould of Harvard; but when it comes to Biblical exegesis GW by-passes Harvard and Yale, Oxford and Cambridge, and puts his money on an obscure theologian (Blocher) in a French provincial seminary. By contrast, Prof. James Barr of Oxford has written:

"... interpretations which suppose that the seven 'days' of creation were not actual days ... are all transparent devices for making the Bible appear to be factually accurate by altering the meaning at the awkward points..."

Quotations

MP blames creationists for quotations 'out of context', but some of his own are scarecely less selective:

1) CS Lewis is summoned as a witness against 'literalism', but in context this passage (MIRACLES p. 96) is showing the difference between statements about Christ ("Son of God") and "events on the historical level" (eg "Jesus turned water into wine"). MP would have done well to ponder CSL's words on the *next* page: "Legitimate 'explanation' degenerates into muddled or dishonest *'explaining away'* as soon as we start applying to these events the metaphorical interpretation which we rightly apply to the statements about God." (my italics)

One wonders what CSL would have made of MP's argument that, because a child might well be confused by

131

Christ's words about 'hating' father and mother, therefore a child's understanding of Genesis must be wrong! 2) Augustine is dragged in (not for the first time) to lend weight to the non-literal theory; but one has only to read his fantastic allegorizations to agree with Luther that they are "extraordinary trifling". Even Davis A. Young, an Old-Earth geologist, admits that until 1800 AD in effect the whole Christian Church believed in a literal 6-Day creation about 6000 years ago.

The Flood Ignored

Considering that it was THE GENESIS FLOOD that sparked off the creation movement 27 years ago (and has run through 28 editions), it is strange to find so few references to the Deluge. No attempt is made to answer Whitcomb & Morris's massive arguments. The Flood is not even mentioned in the 'typical compendium of creationist beliefs' which MP lists in ch. 1 and attempts to refute in ch. 4. Fossils — *the* great problem for evolutionists — are kept well out of sight.

MP & GW apparently hope that their TE approach to Genesis will help unbelievers to treat Christianity with more respect, but evidence from America belies this. In 1986 the ASA sent a 48-page booklet to 60,000 science teachers, to persuade them that 'God works through evolution'. The response of leading American biologists was "almost totally negative". They attacked the booklet as "treacherous", "nefarious", and "pseudo-science" ... "for the ultimate purpose is to coax us to believe in the ASA's particular creation myth." So the compromise-road does not lead to conversions.

Conclusion

So much stress is here laid on the antiquity and "cultural differences" of Genesis that one might easily

132

forget St Paul's assurance that ALL Scripture is profitable, that "whatsoever things were written aforetime were written for OUR learning." Christ's solemn promise in Matthew 5.18 is meaningless if it does not imply the continuity of language and permanent perspicuity of the Old Testament. Add to this the experience of a thousand missionaries that the Bible is "the most translatable book in the world", clearly intended for all nations in all ages. The Reformers' principle was 'interpret Scripture by Scripture', but Poole and Wenham pay no attention to Christ's answer about divorce, St Paul's references to Eve, St Peter's warning about the Flood, and a dozen other NT passages highly relevant to the exegesis of Genesis 1–11. Instead they "torture texts to make them confess the creed of science", and cite only 25 verses outside Genesis.

It will be a great day for Anglican theology when evangelicals awake to the fact that God is no respecter of nations. Today it is the despised American and Australian 'fundamentalists' who have pioneered the research which is toppling the pseudo-science of Lyell and Darwin. Evolution and creation are concepts at least as antithetical as the Mass and Article XXVIII of the Church of England. The Mass was believed by millions, and supported by a towering hierarchy of priests, bishops, cardinals and Popes — but it had to go, because it was "repugnant to the plain words of Scripture". Today evolution is believed by millions and supported by a formidable host of scientists, but it, too, must fall, because it is "repugnant to the plain words of Scripture." Let us hope that Latimer House may soon see the light and — true to their name — join in the Twentieth Century Reformation.

7 *God and Evolution* by R. J. BERRY, Hodder, 189 pp, ISBN 0 340 34249 8 £6.95 (1988)

When a new HISTORY OF THE WARFARE OF SCIENCE WITH THEOLOGY is written for the XXth Century, this book may well be seen as the last *cri de coeur* from an endangered species — the Darwinian "evangelical". One can feel some sympathy for Professor Berry (RB). Here is a man whose whole career is based on the scientific consensus about Origins. From childhood he has been repeatedly told that Darwin is the Newton of biology. In his 20's Sir Julian Huxley was vociferating that "Evolution must now be considered no longer a theory, but a fact." Now, thirty years later, it must be disturbing, at least, for RB to see a tidal wave of new books which threaten to shatter that confidence (see Appendix A).

Worst of all, not one of these books was written from a Christian-apologetic point of view: they are concerned only with scientific *truth* — as was Sir Ernst Chaim when he called evolution "a fairy tale". Attack comes also from the much-maligned "creationists" who assert that the traditional straightforward interpretation of Genesis is the only one that makes sense of the Bible. With his professional reputation at stake, and his integrity as a Christian, RB clutches at every straw that promises hope of survival for Darwinism.

His strategy is to ignore (almost entirely) what he calls "secular criticism" — such as Denton's EVOLUTION: A THEORY IN CRISIS (1985) — and concentrate on ridiculing "creation science". Much of his material is taken uncritically out of American anti-creationist literature: he appears never to have read the Creation Research Society Quarterly, whose articles for 25 years have been up-dating, correcting and improving on the basic work of Whitcomb and Morris. Thus John Lightfoot's alleged pinpointing of creation's date and time — always good for a laugh — has been lifted straight out of A. D. White (1890) who concocted the story by mis-reading the record. The myth was exploded by John Klotz in the CRSQ March 1987, but here we find it coolly resuscitated.

Again, he criticizes Thomas Barnes' (Emeritus Professor of Physics, University of Texas, but RB gives him no credentials!) book on earth-magnetism; but Barnes updated his (1971) book in 1983, 1986 and 1987. RB seems to known nothing of this, and Barnes is not even mentioned in the bibliography. (It is worth pointing out that RB, a natural-scientist, here claims to know more physics than a Professor of Physics, yet scorns all attempts by non-biologists to invade the sacred precinct of Biology). In defence of biological evolution he offers sweeping generalizations by members of his own party, eg Cuffey:

"The fossil record displays numerous sequences of transitional fossils..." but forbears quoting the numerous evolutionists (including Darwin himself) who have said exactly the opposite. Duane Gish is criticized for lumping all 850 species of bat into one 'kind', but RB makes no attempt to trace the pedigree of any *one* species. Evidently Sir Karl Popper's dictum is still right up to date: "Neither Darwin, nor any Darwinian, has so far given an actual causal explanation of any single organism or any single organ." RB cannot resist the temptation to sideswipe (*twice*) poor Philip Gosse whose famous "God created the rocks with fossils already in them" has no relevance whatever to the modern debate (see Whitcomb, THE EARLY EARTH p. 42).

We are glad to note that RB has a high regard for John Calvin, but his quotations from the Reformer are eclectic and very misleading. He makes it appear that Calvin was, or would have been, a supporter of RB's non-literal interpretation of Genesis. In fact JC insists that Adam's *body* was made in a manner quite different from the animals', and roundly rebukes allegorists. RB entangles his argument even worse by quoting the Westminster Confession (1647) in support of his views. As most people know, those excellent divines actually went beyond the Reformers by including:

"It pleased God in the beginning to create the world and all things therein ... *in the space of six days*" (my italics). Could anything be clearer? But RB repeatedly accuses creationists of "deism", banishing God from everyday life, when in fact they believe exactly what our forefathers believed — that He *both* feeds the birds *and* sent the Flood *and* will change our bodies in the (literal) twinkling of an eye.

In his non-literal interpretation RB dismisses as nonsense (quoting Colin Russell) the views of commentators whose knowledge of ancient languages and literature must be fifty times his own. Instead, he quotes at great length Henri Blocher as if he were a new Apostle. Blocher and Berry together are prepared to contradict all the standard commentaries on I Cor.11.8 ("woman is out of the man").

RB also follows Russell in repeating the old, old fallacy, "Darwin's case is a re-run of Galileo's". Is it? Consider: 129 years after Galileo, every European astronomer had accepted the Copernican system. 129 years after Darwin, ten thousand doubts and criticisms remain unanswered. The 'parallel' is hopelessly crooked.

Like many evangelicals, RB thinks he can consistently hold onto the Virgin Birth and NT miracles while at the same time abandoning faith in the Six-Day creation. This is rather naive. J. A. T. Robinson was more logical when he wrote: "Matthew 1 has no more to do with gynaecology than Genesis 1 has to do with geology." Liberal scholars are quick to point out that the Infancy Narratives can be re-interpreted in exactly the same way as RB re-interprets Genesis. "They are not meant to tell us HOW Jesus was born but only WHO he was ..." is a perfect parallel to "Genesis was not intended to teach us HOW God made the world but only WHO did."

Finally RB resorts to psychology: "creationism is a symptom of *fear of a changing future*" (my italics). If only RB had talked to some of these "fearful saints", he might have realised his blunder. As it is, he is content to copy page after page from Americans who try to explain away religious movements in terms of politics and economics. He knows nothing of the success of creationism in Europe, Australia, India, and Korea (where the Association includes 19 University Professors). He asserts that it produces "stunted" Christians, and suggests that St Paul's command to 'be transformed' means swallowing evolution! He would be surprised to find that hundreds of these "stunted" Christians are preaching the Gospel in dark and dangerous corners of the world and (like Henry Martyn, Hudson Taylor, and all the pioneers) teaching their converts to observe the Sabbath *because* God made everything in six literal days.

It is indeed regrettable that one so highly qualified should waste his talents defending the pagan philosophy of which a more mature believer has written:
"St Paul's teaching here is *diametrically opposed to* what is so commonly held ... the *theory of evolution*" (Dr Martyn Lloyd-Jones, EXPOSITION OF ROMANS 8.20) (my italics).

ADDRESSES

BIBLICAL CREATION SOCIETY, PO Box 22, Rugby, Warwicks CV22 7SY
CREATION SCIENCE MOVEMENT, 50 Brecon Avenue, Portsmouth, Hants. PO6 2AW
(slides, books etc.)
SOMERSET CREATION GROUP, Mead Farm, Downhead, Yeovil, BA22 7RQ
(pub. especially for children)
CHRISTIAN WORLD CENTRE, PO Box 30, 123 Deansgate, Manchester M60 3BX
(for ORIGINS films, an excellent series)
THE MUSTARD SEED (creation books) 21 Kentish Town Road, London NW1 8NH

AUSTRALIA:
Creation Science Foundation, PO Box 302, Sunnybank, Qld. 4109 (publishers of a coloured magazine-style quarterly)

USA:
INSTITUTE FOR CREATION RESEARCH, PO Box 2667, El Cajon, CA 92021
(pub. 'Acts & Facts' monthly news bulletin)
CREATION RESEARCH SOCIETY, PO Box 14016, Terre Haute, IN 47803
(pub. a 50-page technical Quarterly)
MASTER BOOKS, PO Box 1606, EL CAJON, CA 92022

***

FOR FURTHER READING

(Master Books)
The Lie: Evolution by Ken Ham

Evolution: The Challenge Of the Fossil Record by Duane Gish
The Natural Sciences Know Nothing of Evolution by Prof. A. E. Wilder-Smith
Man: Ape or Image by Prof. J. Rendle-Short

(Evangelical Press)
Bone of Contention by Sylvia Baker
Concepts in Creationism by Prof. Edgar Andrews et al.
Exposition of Genesis by H. C. Leupold

(Banner of Truth)
Commentary on Genesis by John Calvin

The Moon: Its Creation, Form & Significance
(BMH books, Winona Lake,
   by J. C. Whitcomb & D. B. DeYoung
   Indiana 46590, USA)

139

If you have enjoyed this book, don't forget to read

"MYTHS & MIRACLES"

David Watson here follows up his *GREAT BRAIN ROBBERY*, which was warmly commended by Dr. Martyn Lloyd-Jones, with a detailed commentary on the early chapters of Genesis.

Distilling the essence of many larger books which since 1960 have firmly established Creation as a viable scientific theory, he proposes that

a) nothing in those ancient records is contrary to proven facts.

b) many facts of science and history agree better with a creation dated only thousands of years ago, followed by a world-wide Flood, than with the hypotheses and aeons of Evolution.

The language is non-technical, and Brian Newton's illustrations make this a book to be enjoyed by parents, teachers and children alike.

For classroom use, a number of Projects are suggested to stimulate further study and research.

This book has been printed several times and translated into German, Spanish, and Greek.

David Watson graduated as a senior scholar of Trinity College, Cambridge, in 1947, and has since taught and lectured in India, America and Britain. He is married with three sons.